START YOUR OWN

SPECIALTY
FOOD
BUSINESS

Additional titles in *Entrepreneur's Startup Series*

Start Your Own

Entrepreneur
MAGAZINE'S

 STARTUP

START YOUR OWN

SPECIALTY
FOOD
BUSINESS

YOUR STEP-BY-STEP GUIDE
TO SUCCESS

The Staff of Entrepreneur Media, Inc. & Cheryl Kimball

Ep
Entrepreneur
PRESS®

Entrepreneur Press, Publisher
Cover Design: Andrew Welyczko
Production and Composition: Eliot House Productions

This publication is designed to provide accurate and authoritative information in regard to the
subject matter covered. It is sold with the understanding that the publisher is not engaged in
rendering legal, accounting or other professional services. If legal advice or other expert assistance
is required, the services of a competent professional person should be sought.

Library of Congress Cataloging-in-Publication Data
   Names: Kimball, Cheryl. | Entrepreneur Media, Inc.
   Title: Start your own specialty food business: your step-by-step startup guide to success/
      by The Staff of Entrepreneur Media, Inc. & Cheryl Kimball.
   Description: Irvine : Entrepreneur Press, 2016. | Series: Startup series
   Identifiers: LCCN 2015039453| ISBN 978-1-59918-583-5 (paperback) | ISBN 1-59918-583-0
   Subjects: LCSH: New business enterprises--Management. | Small business. | Food service
      management. | Business planning. | Entrepreneurship.
   Classification: LCC HD62.5 .K536 2016 | DDC 664.0068/1—dc23
   LC record available at http://lccn.loc.gov/2015039453

Printed in the United States of America

20 19 18 17 16   10 9 8 7 6 5 4 3 2 1

Contents

Chapter 5

You've Been Chopped!: Market Research 51

Chapter 6

The Necessary Ingredient: Financing 61

Chapter 7

Home Is Where the Stove Is: Location 75

Chapter 8
All Things Digital. 89

Chapter 9
Chef, Sous-Chef, and Kitchen Help: Employees 99

Chapter 10
How to Not Cook the Books: Accounting 111

Chapter 11
When "To Market" Means Something Else 121

Chapter 12
Social Media. 133

Preface

Starting a specialty food business is not for everyone. Just because you like food, and even if you like to prepare meals for your family or do it regularly for a few friends, making food your business and having food provide you with income is a different kettle of fish.

First, you need to have that entrepreneurial gene or the unwavering desire to start and build a business. There are certainly myriad businesses to get into besides the food business. You can even get into the food business without dealing with food—as a food writer, a supplier of food-business-related items like packaging or marketing services, or building commercial kitchens.

But for real foodies, the actual food is the thing. And for the specialty food foodie, it goes even one step further—taking perhaps everyday food items and making them into something new and exciting, blending flavors or creating astounding presentations.

So, if you can stomach the stress of perishables, swallow the fickleness of the consumer of specialty food, and fortify yourself to keep up with the ever-changing trends in the specialty food category, perhaps the specialty food business is for you and you can create an incredibly rewarding and fun business. Reading this book will help you go into it with your eyes wide open.

The specialty food world is almost literally, as the cliché goes, your oyster. The term "specialty food" covers a wide range of products. The mentors profiled in this book are purveyors of all sorts of specialty foods from toffee and olive oil to sweet potato salsa and gourmet chocolate bars. Specialty food also includes beverages like carbonated drinks, cider, craft beer, and local wine. Then there is yogurt, ice cream, pizza, homemade pasta, organic baby food . . . the list is endless.

And it doesn't stop there. Specialty food can fall not just under what you produce but how you produce it: gluten-free pasta, organic produce, sulfite-free wines. And it can also include how you package it: drinkable yogurt and wine in a box come to mind. It really is an industry that you can enter into under countless umbrellas.

Throughout this book you will see statistics that point to a growing industry. Consumers are becoming more discerning of the food they eat. And with that has come a desire for local and specialty food. As you enter the specialty food industry, you must, however, always keep in mind that a specialty food business is still a business. You may make specialty whoopie pies, which sounds like a heck of a lot of fun, but the bottom line is there is still a bottom line to think about. If you were always the one to make whoopie pies for your friends and family and decide to make a business out of making and selling whoopie pies, you will need to put a different cap on once you start thinking about your whoopie-pie making as a business. All the things that make a business work apply to something as seemingly "fun" as food.

That means you still need to create a solid business plan; you likely need to find funding; location—whether it's a retail shop or a production facility—is critical; employees still are the highest cost of doing business. Add keeping track of inventory and cash-flow issues and trying to fit in all the social media marketing that seems to be a requirement in today's business world, and you will quickly realize that "business" is still the operative word even when it comes to food.

All of the mentors interviewed for this book pointed consistently to planning as a key to success: Make a business plan, plan for a period of time without the business making income, and plan to start your business with more upfront investment than you think you will need. Maybe you even need to plan to plan. If you do more planning than you think is necessary you will go into your business with your eyes open.

As with any business, read everything you can get your hands on and talk with everyone that is even remotely involved with the food business before you spend a dime on your business idea. And, our mentors also consistently mentioned, think about the kind of lifestyle you want to have and make sure your business model fits that lifestyle—there is nothing that will get you more quickly out of the business than creating a business that does not fit your lifestyle and your personality.

Small-business survival statistics haven't changed much. More entrepreneurs than ever opened small businesses in 2014—but, according to the Small Business Administration, about two-thirds of businesses with employees survive at least two years and about half survive at least five years (www.sba.gov/sites/default/files/Business-Survival.pdf). Despite all the odds against a small business lasting, after you read this book you are going to go into it so well prepared and have planned so thoroughly that your specialty food business is going to not only survive but it will also thrive and grow—you will be one of those still around in a decade!

So settle in with a good cup of organically grown herbal tea, some gluten-free crackers smothered in goat cheese, and a few handmade truffles and be prepared to get excited about starting your own specialty food business.

Who Puts the "Specialty" in Specialty Food?

From cheeses, meats, and seafood to shortbreads, toffee, and maple syrup, the specialty food industry has such a wide range of entry points that if you have a food skill and feel passionately about letting others enjoy the fruits of your skill, you should certainly consider taking it to market. And not only is the range of food types broad but you can choose how to participate—as a producer of a specialty food, you can make your product and sell it in your own retail store or via mail order or be strictly a producer providing your product to retail stores or mail order catalogs to sell.

But first, let's look at small business as a whole.

The Current State of Small Business in America

According to the U.S. Census Bureau, small businesses (defined as those with 250 or fewer employees) employ 56.1 million of the nation's private workforce. Firms with fewer than 100 employees make up the largest part of small-business employment.

That said, small business is far from immune to the ups and downs of business cycles. It has taken a while for the small-business sector to recover from the recession in the late 2000s. Just in 2015 did birthing of companies exceed exit rate, a trend not seen since 2007 according to business.com. "Small businesses are the forefront of our economy . . . every minute, a new business in the U.S. is started and according to some people, more than 50

fun fact

This heading probably should be "Eew!" but the Specialty Food Association reports that the next wave in the edible insect market may be cooking oils made from insects. Who knew there even was an "edible insect market"?

▶ State of Small Business

Wasp Barcode is a barcode and system software technology company. Their "State of Small Business Report" (www.waspbarcode.com) found the following statistics:

- ▶ 47 percent of small businesses were more confident in the economy in 2015 than a year before.
- ▶ Product companies were anticipating higher revenue growth than nonproduct companies.
- ▶ 57 percent expected revenue growth in 2015.
- ▶ 56 percent expected to invest less than 3 percent in marketing.
- ▶ 38 percent were expecting to hire employees in 2015.
- ▶ 38 percent planned to spend money on IT in 2015.
- ▶ 35 percent view their company website as very or even extremely important.
- ▶ 54 percent spent over $5,000 in on IT-related equipment and software in 2014.

percent of all workers will be self-employed by 2020." ("The State of Small Business in 2015," May 5, 2015, by Betsy Scuteri, www.business.com.)

The Small Business Administration (SBA)

With statistics like the ones from the U.S. Census Bureau showing that small business (defined as fewer than 250 employees) employ 56.1 million people, it's no wonder the U.S. government has an administration devoted to small businesses. Anyone thinking about starting a business should have the SBA (www.sba.gov) bookmarked for quick access. There is a wealth of information on this site; you couldn't do much better to start your small-business research here.

The SBA started in 1953. It is an independent agency of the federal government helping Americans start and grow small businesses through field offices throughout the U.S. and its territories. The SBA was designed by Congress to also ensure that small businesses get a "fair proportion" of government contracts and sales of surplus property. You can quickly see that using the SBA to its fullest is only to any small business's advantage.

tip

"The global cheese market is expected to surpass the $120 billion mark by 2021, and grow at a combined annual rate of 4 to 4.5 percent over the next six years, according to a recent report by DecisionDatabases. com." Reported in an article titled "Growing Cheese Industry Reveals Opportunities in New Markets" on the Specialty Food website (www. specialtyfood.com).

Through the years, the SBA has met current challenges in the small-business arena such as focusing on minority- and women-owned businesses with special programs and education to help these businesses thrive. They publish the Small Business Resource magazine and annual national resource guides. These resources contain educational information on things like how to apply for a government contract and keep you up-to-date on current legislation and advocacy on behalf of small businesses, as well as some small-business basics like advice on creating a business plan and how to obtain financing.

The SBA was created for you. You will do yourself a favor by referring to their site and contacting them whenever something comes up in the startup phase or as you establish your specialty food small business.

stat fact

With consumers continuing to be health- and wellness-conscious, the demand for specialty foods such as gluten-free baked goods and low-fat snacks continues to rise.

—U.S. Small Business Administration
www.sba.gov

Service Corps of Retired Executives (SCORE)

Imagine 13,000 volunteer mentors at the service of the small-business world. That's what the nonprofit organization SCORE (www.score.org) is all about. There are almost 400 SCORE chapters throughout the U.S. in urban, suburban, and rural communities. Formed in 1964, more than ten million Americans have used SCORE's mentoring services. These mentors can help you at any stage of your business, from planning to startup to growth.

Go to the SCORE website at www.score.org and click on the link to finding a chapter near you. A check of the zip code 03801 (Portsmouth, New Hampshire) produced one chapter right in Portsmouth and five other chapters within a 50-mile range of Portsmouth.

After locating a chapter near you, you submit a request for a mentor, get together with your mentor to get help on specific goals (or help creating specific goals!), and follow up with your mentor throughout the life of your business. SCORE offers online resources that you can sign up for to have emailed to you and they offer local and online workshops and webinars for further education as well as community events such as roundtable discussions and seminars. The website has everything you need to locate all of these services.

warning

Many small-business leaders point to health-care costs along with EPA regulations and increased stringency in OSHA compliance as making it harder and harder to do business today. You shouldn't let this deter you from starting your business, but you should be very aware of these costs as you get started.

The Specialty Food Industry as a Whole

The specialty food industry has far exceeded the realm of the niche market. While some items within the industry may be niche-driven, overall specialty food is itself a force to be reckoned with.

Throughout this book you will hear from those who have done it—a toffee maker who took over the family business; the person with a full-time job who took her hobby of making jams and jellies from local in-season produce and made a side business out of it then put it on hold and has plans to revitalize and expand the business; and the chocolatiers who have a commercial kitchen at their home and added an in-town retail store that they have decided to close.

There are several avenues you can take if you want to start a specialty food business. These include:

- ▶ A homebased business that is self-limiting from not only space but also state and federal food production and sales laws
- ▶ A homebased business that has more opportunity for growth because you have created a commercial kitchen space in your home
- ▶ Your own retail shop that includes a production area
- ▶ Production-only specialty food business that distributes to a network of retailers
- ▶ Production-only specialty food business that focuses on mail order

Of course, a combination of one or two of these is not only a possibility but quite likely. Which is to say that with the specialty food market, the sky's the limit! You need to do some soul searching and figure out some logistics to decide which approach makes sense for you and the business you envision.

Homebased

The SBA offers the following five steps to help you decide if a homebased specialty food business is right for you:

1. Ensure that you and your home are properly equipped for the business of food production. What do you intend to produce? Do you have the equipment? Do you fall within the limits of local zoning laws?
2. Finance your homebased business. The SBA does not give out loans but they do have a guaranty program with banks and lenders that you should check

warning

The food industry is heavily regulated in every state. Do not ignore these laws. In New Hampshire, one of the general laws about food stores (RSA 143-A:4) reads: "It shall be unlawful for any person, unless exempted under RSA 143-A:5, to operate a food service establishment or retail food store within the state without having obtained a food service license to be issued by the [DHHS] commissioner. For new establishments or establishments that change ownership, an application must be submitted along with the appropriate fee and an inspection must be conducted before a license will be issued."

out. Their Microloan program guarantees loans averaging $13,000 with the high side at $35,000.

3. Take the appropriate steps to license and register your homebased business. It is not worth it to try to skirt around the regulations. You do not want to risk your business.

4. Understand the regulations that govern food production. Again, you need to know what you are required to do and you need to do it. It is not worth risking all your hard work trying to skirt around regulations that just seem too difficult. Contact your county's public health department and find out all you need to know.

5. Marketing your food product or service online. Don't look at the internet as regulation-free. The food business has very specific regulations governing online ordering and marketing of food, known in general as "ecommerce," much of which, the SBA says, is state-regulated. If you plan to sell across state lines it gets even more complicated. Find out what these regulations are before betting your whole business on online sales.

> **aha!**
>
> Who says your specialty foods business has to be food for humans? The pet food business is a booming one. Pet owners are spending billions each year on Fido and Fifi. Buying them special homemade treats is one aspect of that booming market. Perhaps you find pet specialty food a more appealing market or perhaps you can add it as a sideline to your specialty-food-for-people retail store.

The Retail Store

Starting and running a retail store is an animal all its own and one that, according to the SBA, more than a quarter million people in the U.S. earn a living doing. The SBA offers the following tips to get you off on the right foot:

▶ *Determine which type of retail model is right for you.* If you have decided on a physical store as opposed to online retailing, you might want to consider whether there is an existing store for sale that would meet your plans. If you are going to start from scratch, be sure to check all the regulations for retailing the specific type of specialty food you are planning to create.

▶ *Find the right location.* As we discuss in more detail in Chapter 7, you need your location to be where your target market goes. The SBA recommends making sure to "combine visibility, accessibility, affordability, and commercial lease terms that you can live with."

▶ *Finance your retail venture.* In other words, make sure you have the proper financial backing to fund your startup until the business starts to earn income. This is one of the key reasons that small business startups do not make it. Chapter 6 walks you through financing.

▶ *Determine your business structure.* Do you want to head out alone or do you think a partnership of some kind might make it more likely for your business to succeed? While you can certainly hire employees to staff a retail store, a partner will ease that burden and fill in other skills that you lack or are not interested in. Choose a partner who complements your own skill set. Partnerships can go sour very easily, but if you do your upfront due diligence, it might end up being the best decision you make for the success of your business.

▶ *Take care of the regulatory requirements involved in starting and operating a business.* The food business has some unique and strict regulations that you will want to be sure to know and adhere to. If your retail store has a production area, you need to know the regulations for two very different aspects of your business.

Production and Distribution

You may decide that a retail store is just not right for you. You have decided that you will produce your specialty food but leave it to others more suited to retail to sell it for you. Your product still has to get to the retail stores, and the stores need to know about your product, so there is a still a lot to do besides produce your specialty food.

If the idea of marketing and the organizational details of marketing, selling, and shipping don't appeal to you, you had better plan to find someone to whom that does appeal, because getting those three things right will make or break your business. You can produce all the great product in the world but if no one knows you have it, and no one sells it for you, your business is going nowhere.

Production

The actual siting of a production operation is covered in Chapter 7, but to make the initial decision to do the production and let others do the selling, you need to focus on getting that production facility just right. First, as already stated, make sure you check with state regulations about a production facility. One of the mentors in this book decided to create her own commercial kitchen at her house—she found the process went very smoothly from planning the kitchen to its passing state inspection because she did some upfront work of having the regulators in her state help her before anyone pounded a nail to create the kitchen. You should do the same with your production facility.

You can choose to buy an existing facility or build out your own. It can be on the outskirts of town in a strip mall (these facilities are usually designed to be very flexible in renovating interior space) or in a warehouse area in your town or even at your own home if you have the space. It is often best to locate near your target market. In order to determine where that might be, use Figure 1–1: Target Market Worksheet. But no matter where you choose to locate, the

stat fact

Small businesses created 108,000 jobs in March of 2015.

—ADP Payroll Services

Target Market Worksheet

How well have you defined your target market? This list can help you get organized and coordinate your efforts:

Identify three specialty areas you would like to target:

1. _____

_____

2. _____

_____

3. _____

_____

What specific skills do you have in those areas?

_____

_____

_____

_____

_____

FIGURE 1–1: **Target Market Worksheet**

Will you need additional training or education?

_____

_____

What additional equipment will you need?

_____

_____

_____

Identify your clients:

_____

_____

_____

Who is your competition?

_____

_____

_____

How will your business be different?

_____

_____

_____

Is your geographic location favorable to your business?

_____

_____

_____

FIGURE 1–1: **Target Market Worksheet,** continued

regulations for the inside of the production facility will be the same. Be sure to find out what they are.

Marketing

Once you have your production facility planned and you know when you expect to start rolling out your first product, you will need to make sure to start marketing to the retailers that you hope will sell your product. Be prepared to provide samples to potential retailers. You can run a sample batch of your product (even if you have to rent a commercial kitchen for that). You can send samples to potential retailers or attend a trade conference where retailers check out wholesaler booths/products (check www.specialtyfood.com for one in your region).

However you decide to approach retailers, be sure to send the product in the actual packaging you plan to use so they can see the finished product and how it will look on their store shelves. If you are not 100 percent sure of the finished packaging, use potential retailers as an unofficial focus group and ask their opinions about different packaging possibilities.

Distribution

You've landed several retailers around the region, or even the country (be sure you are legal, food-safety-wise, in every state you plan to do business!), to carry your product. Now you need to get it to them. This is where you need to decide on the best shipping method to ensure your product gets to the retailer intact, the way you intend it to look. One of the mentors in this book has decided not to invest in all the hot-weather packaging required to ensure safe delivery of their chocolate bars; therefore, they do not ship during the hottest season. They do not want their carefully created beautiful chocolate bars to arrive "as a puddle of chocolate." You don't want something like that to happen either.

Mail order specialty food retailer Omaha Steaks has created a shipping model for their frozen meats to ensure safe delivery. Their products ship via overnight mail and are flash frozen with dry ice inside a Styrofoam shipping cooler. Recipients are instructed on the outside packaging to unpack and put the contents in the freezer as soon as possible.

Not only do you need to decide on distribution range and packaging, but your facility needs to be able to accommodate the packing and shipping process. This is a whole different animal from creating the specialty food you plan to sell, so, once again, if this is not something that revs you up to get

tip

One way to decide how you need to distribute your products is from the bottom line income your business needs to make to succeed. If you have the base in your region to meet that goal without casting your net wider—great. You can always expand later. Do keep in mind that many retailers do not appreciate it if you spread your product so widely in the region that sales outlets are cutting into each other's sales totals.

► Retail Secrets You Should Know

Here are a few things, according to the Retail Doctor's Blog ("41 Things No One Told You About Starting a Retail Business" at www.retaildoc.com) that might surprise you:

- ► As soon as you figure out what your customers want, they will want something totally different.
- ► People in your town will assume you are rich because you have your own business.
- ► You will work weekends and holidays; if you don't like it, don't go into retailing.
- ► Sometimes a Tuesday might be your best day; other times it will be a Saturday. In this business, there is often no consistency.
- ► The customer is always right.
- ► You will rarely have a for sure day off again.
- ► Just because someone asks for a discount doesn't mean they won't buy if you don't give them one.
- ► Running a business is harder than you think it'll be, but you won't really have time to notice.

If you find these helpful and interesting, go to www.retaildoc.com to read the other 33.

out of bed and get to work each morning, make sure you hire someone who has the skill to get an efficient distribution process underway and operating.

Other Specialty Food Venues

Perhaps you have an idea for a specialty food that you feel could make a business but the thought of producing food and getting it to the consumer through the retail market or mail order doesn't quite suit you. There are several other ways you could get into the specialty food business.

Strictly Special Order

You could make your specialty food—say it's chocolates or lollipops or cake pops or goat cheese formed in the shape of a goat—and simply sell it via special orders. Corporate gifts to put in gift baskets, maybe those famous baskets of high-end items that the stars get in their hotels at the Academy Awards ceremony, wedding receptions, other big parties—the list of possibilities is endless. In this kind of business, you would have to have samples to offer, but your product is always presold. You would still need a production facility. You could lease a commercial kitchen, but then you would still have to put it all together somewhere—plate it, wrap it, box it, however you plan to present it to your client.

The other thing about this approach is that you will either need to spend as much time on sales as on making your food item or you will need to hire someone (or take on a partner) to do the sales part for you.

Food Truck

Food trucks continue to be hot in certain parts of the country. They tend to do well either on Main Street where there are a lot of people or in rural areas where lunch options are few and far between.

A food truck is a great place to sell certain specialty food concoctions—from special creations like veggie hot dogs with your special homemade sauerkraut or gourmet pretzels with a variety of dipping sauces or fruit dipped in different chocolate and sauces, crepes, meatballs, cupcakes—the possibilities are nearly limitless.

warning

Even though you are operating out of a food truck, there are still plenty of health and food safety regulations you must follow as well as general licensing fees and fees specific to your vending operation. Check local and state regulations for the laws specific to where you will be operating.

There are many advantages and unique features to food trucks. Here are a few, according to "Food Trucks 101: How to Start a Mobile Food Business" by Entrepreneur Press and Rich Mintzer (www.entrepreneur.com/article/220060):

▶ You can choose a variety of locations from street corners to train and bus stations to resorts and conference centers, corporate parking lots, even beachside (how fun is that?).

▶ 78 percent of food trucks have four or fewer employees.

▶ The mobile unit can be moved if you find the area you set up in isn't as busy as you thought it might be.

▶ The food trucks themselves have become capable of housing very sophisticated equipment.

There are, says the article from Entrepreneur Press, two different kinds of food trucks:

1. The MFPV, or "mobile food preparation vehicle," where food is prepared as the customer waits

2. The ICV, or "industrial catering vehicle," which sells only prepackaged food—sort of a vending machine with lots more choices

Of course, the ICV tends to be cheaper than the MFPV—which could run upwards of $100,000—because the unit where food is prepared needs lots more equipment. The food cart is the cheapest of all, likely costing under $3,000 for a used one.

Don't get duped into thinking the food truck business is easy! It may be "easier" than opening a storefront or a distribution center, but it has its own quirks. As most of our mentors point out in Chapter 3, you need to figure out what kind of business suits your personality and lifestyle preference.

Some things to keep in mind are:

▶ Staffing the food truck itself is likely to only be a small portion of your day. Prep, office work like ordering supplies, and picking up supplies typically takes a couple hours of the day before and/or after the truck itself is in operation on-site.

▶ Cleanup is key. Your food truck needs to be as neat and clean as any other food operation.

warning

Food trucks have the unique issue of being out in the weather. You can create a food truck that keeps you comfortable in most conditions, but how likely are your customers to stand in line in a blizzard? You need to account for those days when you just can't set up shop. This can be difficult for people who like regularity and need to count on that income every day.

▶ Getting to and from your destination can take time. Of course, ideal is if you can keep your truck on-site even if it means packing it up and moving it a few hundred yards. But you may then fall under some different regulations since you are technically not a mobile truck unit if you don't move.

▶ Marketing doesn't go away just because you are mobile. Unless, and even if, you are set up in a busy downtown area, people need to know about you. Social media can be great promotion for this kind of food business.

Entrepreneur and Mintzer's article estimates that if you take an average of $60,000 for purchase of a food truck and add:

▶ $1,000 for startup ingredients;

▶ $2,000 for permits and licenses;

▶ $2,000 for the first month's rental of a commercial kitchen;

▶ $300 for the first month of parking and truck maintenance;

▶ $2,000 for packaging;

▶ $1,000 for your home office for bookkeeping, etc.;

▶ and $500 for miscellaneous costs,

You can get into the food truck business for just under $75,000. And if in a few months it isn't what you thought it would be, you can likely recoup a lot of your vehicle costs by selling it used to the next person who thinks he wants to give the food truck business a try!

tip

Decide where and what time you want to set up shop and stick with it for a while. It takes time for people to get accustomed to your presence and tell their friends where they are getting their great lunch or midafternoon snack and coffee. You don't want to keep them guessing about where you are going to be!

Personal Chef

Being a personal chef for people on a specialty diet can be a very rewarding way to get into specialty food. Cancer patients, especially those on chemotherapy, can really benefit from a personal chef who knows how to make food that is especially appealing when chemotherapy drugs make food unappealing but when it is important to maintain nutrition for strength and the best health possible. James Haller, former chef in Portsmouth, New Hampshire, who ran the locally famous gourmet restaurant The Blue Strawberry and is credited with establishing the now vigorous Portsmouth restaurant scene, became engaged in food specifically for cancer patients, including writing the book *What to Eat When You Don't Feel Like Eating* (Robert Pope Foundation, 1994).

Other types of specialty cooking for health reasons include:

▶ Low-sodium and other high-blood pressure-related nutrition
▶ Diabetes and low-sugar diets
▶ Heart disease and low-fat, low-cholesterol cooking
▶ Celiac disease and gluten-free cooking

Besides being personal chef for those with chronic diseases, you can also get into specialty cooking as a personal chef for working couples with children who feel like they don't have time to cook healthfully for the family. Or for those who are in positions to host frequent parties, events, and social functions who want someone they can count on to come into their home, take over the kitchen, and wow their guests with food within whatever budget they set for you.

There are some extra credentials you will need or want to successfully promote yourself in the specialty food personal chef business for those with chronic illnesses or health dietary concerns. This may be as little as having a go-to consultant in the medical field for that particular chronic health issue. Or you may want to get some training yourself in the specific field. The diabetes category, for instance, has a very formalized segment in the industry on diabetes education. Registered dietitians can specialize in any of these fields. And while you may not want to do the rigorous education for becoming an R.D., they often work independently and you can line them up as consultants. Contact the Academy of Nutrition and Dietetics (formerly the American Dietetic Association) at www.eatright.org to find registered dietitians near you.

Retail Food Store Regulations

Once you start thinking about combining the food industry and retail, you have a lot to think about. Check with the state in which you plan to do business to get the most up-to-date information about the laws and regulations you need to abide by to prepare and sell food to the public. In New Hampshire, for instance, you would check with the Department of Health and Human

stat fact

According to Statista (www.statista.com), specialty food store revenues in the United States in 2010 totaled almost $8 billion.

fun fact

According to the Specialty Food Association, botanicals such as ginger in beverages is a growing trend, especially in European markets. In the first three quarters of 2015, 12.7 percent of carbonated soft drink launches in the U.K. contained ginger compared to 3.3 percent in 2010. Does what starts in Europe become a U.S. trend? Perhaps someone might try it and find out!

Services. An online search of "selling food in New Hampshire" brings you to the DHHS site where there is information about licensing mobile food units, food sanitation, and more. Some regulations you may encounter include:

▶ To establish a food service business or food store in New Hampshire you must, among other things, submit a Food Establishment Floor Plan with a fee, which as of this writing is $75.

▶ Not only do you need to submit the floor plan, a water system plan, and a wastewater plan, but you also must include information that is required of all new retail establishments and businesses.

▶ If you plan to buy or sell a food service establishment or retail food store you must submit at least 30 days in advance a list of several items to the Food Protection Program including the establishment's license, written request for the change, a letter from the most recent owner acknowledging the impending transfer, as well as a floor plan checklist, water systems compliance plan, and wastewater system compliance plan—and any fees of course!

▶ Look into the requirements from the Food Sanitation Inspection and Licensing Program, which will do routine inspections and investigate complaints. They also will help train food service workers, and they issue 90-day provisional licenses to new businesses and those that have changed ownership.

Every state has different laws that may be administered and regulated by different departments, or even more than one department. The onus is on you to do the proper research and contact departments and get the licensing you need to legally operate a retail food store in your state.

The bottom line is there are a lot of angles to think about when opening a specialty food business—and many of them are not specifically about food! But the specialty food industry is well entrenched in the U.S. retail consumers' minds and can be well worth the effort to get your unique or same-old, same-old just more excellent than what is out there food business off the ground.

Sites to Know

To work with food you will want to become as familiar as you can with food safety standards as mandated by the FDA. Bookmark these websites:

warning

If you are dealing with liquor on any level be sure to check with your state's liquor commission to find out what rules you need to follow with regard to liquor sales or consumption.

▶ *www.foodsafety.gov.* A dissemination site billed as "Your Gateway to Federal Food Safety Information." Here you will find safety alerts such as salmonella outbreaks and the latest news regarding food safety and handling. This is primarily a consumer-oriented website, but it is well organized and comprehensive.

▶ *www.fsis.usda.gov.* This is the website for the Food Safety and Inspection Service and is another place to find the latest news regarding food safety, recalls, and other food-related public health concerns.

▶ *www.fda.gov.* Mentioned several times in this book, this is the site for the U.S. Food and Drug Administration. You can register here online as a food facility that manufactures, processes, packs, or holds food for either human or animal consumption. There is also information about labeling, packaging, additives, and other guidance.

▶ *www.usda.gov.* This site has a "food and nutrition" section that includes general information on things such as the food pyramid and child nutrition as well as information on food safety, recalls, security issues, and other food-related news.

stat fact

Seventy percent of consumers in the age group of 25 to 34 were likely to purchase specialty foods, according to Statista. Next were 18- to 24-year-olds at 69 percent, followed by 35- to 44-year-olds at 60 percent. The lowest rank was among those over 65, but even still that was a respectable 45 percent, which is a lot of consumers considering the over-65 crowd represents a large percentage of the baby boom generation.

You Like to Eat but Is this Business Right for You?

Deciding whether or not the food business is the right business for you is critical to your success once you do get into it. A lot of time and likely considerable expense goes into creating a thriving food business. There may be a little bit of luck too, but if anyone tells you a lot of it is luck, don't listen. A lot of the success in specialty foods is from excellent, detailed planning and good old-fashioned hard work to make your plan a reality.

Test Yourself

One of the best ways to find out if a business fits your personality and lifestyle is to work in it for a while before plunging in and setting up your own shop. If you are in a full-time job, there are many possibilities for part-time work in the specialty food business. It can be educational just to take a part-time temporary position in a chocolate shop during the busy holidays or pull an evening shift two or three nights per week at a production facility. Maybe you are looking at craft beer, or cider, or wine as a potential business; even a couple of shifts a week as a bartender at a small brewery can get you in the atmosphere of the small brew business to get a sense of what to expect. Plus you can earn a little extra cash while you are at it to add to the business startup piggy bank!

fun fact

Pop-up stores (retail shops that open in an empty space just for a season) are said to be perfect for millennials who "value new experiences over ownership or possession of products," says Werner van Huffelen, owner of The Design Strategist in the Netherlands ("The Power of the Pop-up Business" by Alexandra Gibbs, www. cnbc.com, 8/21/15).

When you work in a similar job or as you get started in planning your business, think about the following:

▶ Do the typical hours mesh with your preferred lifestyle? If you are interested in opening a craft beer brewery, do you need to be up late at night when being a night owl isn't your usual style? Bakeries tend to get started early in the morning; is the phrase "early riser" one that has never been part of your vocabulary?

▶ If you have always been accustomed to taking off on a trip whenever the spirit moves you, opening a retail shop is probably not a good match for you. Perhaps a production setup in a category that has a couple of extremely busy seasons and then slower periods where you could shut down for a week at a time would work better for you.

▶ Someone with a gregarious personality might not want to open a one-person production business where you are by yourself all the time. And someone who is not fond of spontaneous interactions with strangers is not a good candidate to open and run a retail storefront.

This is not to suggest that every possible aspect of a food business can be self-selected around your personal idiosyncrasies. But don't set yourself up to get into a business type that is just going to make you regret your decision, dread going to work, or not feel like putting a 110 percent effort into your new business. That is a recipe for failure before you even begin.

Of course, all of this is moot if you have a business that can afford to hire employees to do everything you don't particularly enjoy doing. But that is atypical of a startup business of any kind, and certainly of one in the specialty food industry.

Small-Business Personality Traits

There are six traits that are conducive to small-business success according to an article by Ben Popper in *Business Insider* called "Six Personality Traits Every Small-Business Owner Should Have" (January 13, 2011). The article disseminates the results of a study by the Guardian Life Small Business Research Institute which found "that there were certain traits that stood out among the most successful ventures." These six traits are:

1. *Being collaborative.* Know when and how to delegate and motivate others on staff.
2. *Curiosity.* Have an interest in scouring the world for ways to improve your business.
3. *Focusing on the future.* Business owners that plan cash flow and succession planning do better.
4. *Self-fulfilled.* Those who would rather be in control of their own destiny than feel secure in a corporate environment are more successful.
5. *Tech-savvy.* It's here, it's the world, use it to your advantage and make your business more efficient.
6. *Action-oriented.* Adversity actually makes strong business leaders work harder and motivates them.

One group (RingCentral) reporting on this study in a blog post actually pulled "desire to delegate" from the

warning

Don't get a job to test the waters within the same market you plan to set up in. Drive at least a couple towns away—you don't want your potential competitors to think you were spying on them. Getting the inside story about a competitor is not your intention; your intention is to get the inside experience.

tip

If your small business will have employees, now's the time to start learning about leadership. "A good leader allows both employee responsibility and creativity to encourage growth and new ideas." ("5 Leadership Lessons from Successful Small-Business Owners" by Royale Scuderi, Open Forum, www.americanexpress.com)

▶ Using Trends to Your Advantage

Some basic trends mentioned in the article "Finding the Right Small Business for You" from www.bizfilings.com that are worth keeping in mind as you make decisions about your business are:

1. Both husbands and wives are wage earners in today's market. This means that tasks that were once commonly performed by a stay-at-home wife/mom (like meal preparation) are often now delegated. Is this a service you can provide?

2. Outsourcing is popular in today's businesses. Employees have been laid off and outsourced replacements brought in. Is there something in this trend that you can capitalize on? Maybe not in the specialty food business, but being creative is the name of the game.

3. Is there a technological approach that you could make a business from? What if you spent an hour on your computer in the early evening and offered 10 people to email you what they have in their fridge and you suggest a meal to them? Even technology is creative!

Be sure to spend time interacting with the community. Join in on sidewalk sales and demo days. Attend chamber of commerce events and offer to bring samples of your product. Join the local Rotary Club and interact with business leaders who can bring business your way. These are some ways you can expand a retail operation into much more than the four walls of your shop.

"being collaborative" trait and thought it was important enough to be a trait of its own. It is probably unlikely that any one person is strong in all these traits. But think them through and think about your own approach to any one of them. Then figure out how you might strengthen the ones you are weaker in, even if the solution is something like delegating to someone else to be tech-savvy!

Other Things to Consider

The food business is a category like no other. While a specialty food business does not have the pressures of the restaurant industry, there are similar things to consider.

stat fact

According to the Census Bureau, women own 36 percent of all U.S. businesses, and of those, 89 percent have no employees.

The Pressure of Perishables

Dealing with food often means dealing with perishable products—whether it is the product you make or the ingredients you need to make the product. Keeping track of your inventory and your product is a key chore for the food business owner. You need to be meticulous in your records and with your ordering process. It is somewhat simpler today to do "just in time" ordering, but that has to be balanced with making sure you have what you need to take on that sudden huge order that could give your business the best week ever—if only you had 200 pounds of flour on hand.

You can fill in with purchasing at one of the big box stores, but you may find it means less profit on your big order, and sometimes it might mean compromising the quality of your ingredients, which is probably not worth it. It helps to find a couple of foodie business friends and set up a network where you can help each other out in these kinds of circumstances.

The other aspect of perishables is that what you don't sell in your retail store becomes day-old after a day. For some items the shelf life is a bit longer than a day. This is an issue for baked goods. Some of it you can deal with by packaging for longer life. Bakeries and other best-when-fresh food purveyors can set up with a nonprofit soup kitchen to deliver any unused food at the end of the day; the food is still good, it just might not present well for customers to purchase. There might be other nonprofits who might be able to use that day's unsold goods at an evening meeting or event. And you might even be able to write off those donations.

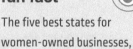

fun fact

The five best states for women-owned businesses, according to Thumbtack, are:

1. New Hampshire
2. Texas
3. Kansas
4. Oklahoma
5. Colorado

Whatever you do, you need to figure out if you can handle the pressure that comes with perishables and if you have the organizational and planning to skills to order as closely as possible so that you can sell most of what you make.

Deadlines

The specialty food business you have in mind may be a chocolate shop—a small storefront with a production area in back. You get up in the morning and make whatever confection you fancy making that day. Your customers love coming in to see what you've come up with to join the solid-selling standbys. But if you also make your business work by taking orders for special occasions, be prepared to work under deadline pressures.

▶ Choose the Right Business for You

In the online article "Finding the Right Small Business for You," Bizfilings' Business Owner's Toolkit (www.bizfilings.com) offers the following three common mistakes that people make in choosing a business (and reasons that often result in business failure):

1. Not doing the right amount of market research on demand for a product or service that is currently your hobby that you "think would make a good business"

2. Not planning enough

3. Not asking for help

Don't succumb to these pitfalls. There is plenty of information out there on small-business startups in general, on specific types of businesses, and certainly on the specialty food industry. Read everything you can get your hands on, call people, network and actually contact the people that come as a result of your networking, and ask for help from those who have been there and from the professionals who are in the business of helping small businesses.

You are the owner and you can decide how you want to work—set up your business in a way that doesn't make it unpleasant to go to work each day! This may mean doing something a little different from what you originally had in mind. With a small business, this is not just a job, it's your life!

The Waiting Game

Retail is retail no matter what you are selling. Retail means having a shop in which you sit waiting for customers to come in and buy your stuff. You can always hire someone to staff your retail store, but that just means that you are paying someone else to sit in a shop and wait for customers to come in and buy your stuff. This is why several of the mentors interviewed for this book were not at all interested in opening a retail outlet for their product—Yummy Yammy owner Lisa Johnson did not even consider opening a retail store for her sweet potato salsa; Seattle toffee maker Susan Burns lets other retailers carry her product and the extent of her retail interaction is to do several demos in those stores; Winnipesaukee Chocolates owners Jonathan Walpole and his wife Sally opened a retail shop a few years into their chocolate-making business only to decide a few years into it that they no longer wanted to be tied down to the store and they didn't want the expense of hiring someone to staff it for them.

► The Factory Model versus the Fruit Stand Model

George Horrigan, business planner and founder of Foundationhead Consulting Group and author of business books including *Creating a Thriving Business* (Morgan James, 2013), talks about the "factory model versus the fruit stand model" of growing a business. Almost all businesses start out in the "fruit stand model," where the owner is highly involved and opens the doors in the morning, and if the owner is not there the business does not make money. And some businesses are naturally in the fruit stand mode longer than others. But for those business owners with the goal of expanding or eventually having their business work for them, Horrigan encourages establishing their businesses with the intention of quickly moving to the "factory model" where the owner is dealing with the bigger picture issues that lead to a thriving business and sets up processes where day-to-day business can be delegated to others. This is what Horrigan feels leads to a thriving business that is set up to grow from the beginning.

But for many people, retail is their dream. All this is fine if retail is what you want for your business—although it is probably rare for small retailers to get wealthy, many retail business owners make a sufficient living and love the retail shop atmosphere and interacting with customers.

Also, retail can (and probably should) be much more than sitting waiting for customers. You will want to use your retail shop as a home base for your business and spend time soliciting large-order customers. You can try out new packaging and new products on basically an impromptu focus group of the people who happen to wander in the door that week.

aha!

Each year, Thumbtack (an online service matchmaker) rates U.S. cities for their small-business friendliness. The five worst for 2015 were:

1. Hartford, CT
2. Albuquerque, NM
3. Buffalo, NY
4. New Haven, CT
5. Winston-Salem, NC

⁙ Meet Your Mentors

There is no better way to learn the ins and outs of starting any small business than to talk with business owners who have done it—either successfully or not. In fact, sometimes those who have not been successful are the ones you can learn from the most!

The following specialty food businesses are still in operation. You will see that their owners are passionate about what they do. They will occasionally be mentioned in other parts of this book with tips in pertinent chapters specific to a topic. Therefore it seems appropriate that you meet them near the beginning of this book so when they are quoted later you'll already be acquainted.

Confectionately Yours Toffee

Susan Desjardins Burns' husband's aunt developed a toffee recipe in the '70s in the Seattle area and sold it wholesale as well as in her candy store. In her 80s, she was still making the toffee which had become popular. But while the toffee was up to its usual standard, the 80-year-old candy maker started to let business-related things like licenses lapse. Aunt Lila was ready to give up the business and offered to let Susan and her husband take the recipe and continue the family tradition.

When it became clear that Susan would be the toffee maker, she began to get her arms around the business. "There was a little guilt factor," Susan admits with a smile. "You have to do this or my toffee recipe will die with me." Susan, a nurse by training, was not a baker, not a chef. Aunt Lila taught her everything. "I changed only one thing about the recipe," she says. "I use agave nectar instead of high fructose corn syrup."

That was in 2005. Five years passed and the toffee was making a profit and she was able to save a little money. Up to that point, Susan had been renting space in a commercial kitchen, which meant it was a shared space. "I found that hard," she says. So she used her five years of success and savings and built her own commercial kitchen in a garage at their home.

In Washington State, the Department of Agriculture regulates wholesalers. Susan contacted them to look at her space before she spent the $24,000 it took to build the commercial kitchen. The representatives gave her some advice on how to do it. The kitchen was designed to be sealed from the garage and with its own entrance.

She filed her paperwork and design to the state. "There were fees, but I didn't feel they were excessive," she says. Susan feels this upfront interaction with the regulators prior to building seemed to make the process work better. Some of the regulations are a little vague and she was able to get clarifications—for instance, whether a floor drain was needed, which would require some excavation. Her plan was approved in record time, she built her kitchen, and she is now very pleased with that decision. "I know what is going on in my kitchen," Susan says.

Confectionately Yours has no other employees besides Susan. "It is too much expense and I feel you lose quality," she says. Her college-aged daughter created the company website. The only printed materials she has are business cards. Her main marketing is doing demos at each one of her retail outlets four times per year. This helps her remain on their minds in a competitive market where stores are trying new stuff all the time.

"I wasn't keen on it at first," Susan admits about taking on Confectionately Yours, "but now I love it. I love being self-employed."

Kitchen Debauchery Jams and Jellies

The first time Joni Van Gelder cooked, it was at 12 years old as an au pair for five children. The only thing she knew how to cook were grilled Velveeta cheese sandwiches. She expanded her repertoire to spaghetti and meatballs and kept expanding it as the kids grew older.

Years later, she married a man who was raised in Holland and Mexico. Her mother-in-law was well-traveled and had culinary expectations of her daughter-in-law, showing her how to prepare meals and fancy appetizers. "This got me interested in learning about cooking," Joni says.

The company she now works for has annual themed parties, and the first time she contributed food, the company got wind of Joni's cooking skills. They started hiring her to cook for the party. Then she started getting catering jobs.

"My shortcoming," she says about taking this catering gig further, "was that I did not have the kitchen to do a catering business from my home. I couldn't do it above board [with the food licenses necessary] so I didn't do it."

At some point Joni added jam and jelly making to her growing list of food talents. "I started going to local farm stands and picking massive amounts of fruit." She started making her own jam and giving it away as gifts. People loved it and asked for more. At one point Joni wondered, "Why the heck am I giving it away?" An accounting friend offered to do a pro forma business P & L, and Kitchen Debauchery was born.

The Homestead Act had just been passed allowing an easier entry into homebased food businesses that dealt in foods that were not considered risks and had other criteria for keeping businesses small. Joni documented everything so if anyone had questions she had plenty of backup.

A Kitchen Debauchery newsletter went out regularly. She created a price list. And mostly the business was a success. But a full-time job, a couple of new grandchildren, and the inability to expand the business without considerable expense has left Kitchen Debauchery on the sidelines for the time being.

The exciting news for Joni is that she is in the midst of designing a new house to put on her New Hampshire lakeside lot. While Joni isn't building a new house just to have an expanded kitchen, it is definitely a benefit that would allow her to take the business to the next level. This is what is taking up her free time at the moment.

Besides truly believing in yourself and your product, Joni advises not starting out too big and not overwhelming yourself from the start. "Think as small as you can, then cut that in half," Joni advises about starting a small specialty food business. "It's like adding salt to soup—you can always expand."

Lincoln Olive Oil Shop

Lincoln Olive Oil Shop owner Rob Baker initially hooked up with some shop owners in Colorado for whom an olive oil shop was working well. They had shops in Fort Collins and Boulder. Using that model, Rob opened his shop in Lincoln, Nebraska, whose historic Haymarket district offered a similar venue to those in which the Colorado shops were doing so well. "We tweaked a few things for the local market," Rob says, but otherwise the setup for his store is basically the same as the ones he learned from. Everything comes to them wholesale and they bottle in the store; 7 to 8 percent of their sales are from online orders and another 7 percent from offsite events.

The store itself is organized as a tasting bar—customers get a free guided tasting tour around the store, testing olive oils from traditional 18-year-aged to oils infused with things like garlic to dark chocolate and cranberry pear.

Rob advises specialty retail startups to never underestimate the importance of location. "On Saturdays, the largest farmers' market in the Midwest wraps around the front and back door of the store," he explains. "No matter what your business, location is critical."

Rob tried a shop in Omaha in a mall location, but the sales were not good enough to pay for the costs associated with being in a mall. The Lincoln Haymarket location has worked perfectly.

In his kind of business, Rob also explains, you have to do more than just turn the "closed" sign to "open" each morning. At $20 per bottle, his olive oil is not an inexpensive purchase. It's important to educate customers so that they are confident in buying your product and knowing how to use it. To that end, they have both public and private cooking classes at the store. They conduct off-site events as well to speak about their olive oils and the services the shop provides. And on top of all that, they have a nonprofit fundraising program. If that isn't enough, to add to the shop's appeal, Lincoln Olive Oil Shop also carries a wide variety of other gourmet items such as cheese, pasta, spices, and a wide variety of sauces focusing on Nebraska-made where possible.

A store like this is labor-intensive from a customer service standpoint, so staffing is key. "You need to provide customers with a total experience," Rob explains. He has employees, especially over the busy holiday season and on the Saturday farmers' market days.

Rob has a background in marketing and feels that marketing is not only something he is skilled at but is critical for the shop's success. "For 12 years I opened new stores for Walmart," he says. "When you open a Walmart store, people just come. That's not true with a small specialty food business." Surprisingly even to him, Rob has found newspapers to be the best advertising medium for Lincoln Olive Oil. He has joined a unique program with the *Lincoln Journal Star* where they offer a weekly deal to readers. For $25 consumers get a $50 gift certificate to the business featured that week. The consumer sends the money to the newspaper and the featured business gets dollar-for-dollar value in advertising in the paper. Lincoln Olive Oil honors the gift certificates and gets exposure to new customers and the potential of the customers redeeming the certificate buying more than the gift certificate's value. And of course the net cost to him is much less than the retail value of the $50. It's a win-win in Rob's eyes.

They stopped radio advertising but continue advertising on TV only on the ABC affiliate during the daytime foodie show, *The Chew*. By focusing, Rob says, the results are tenfold over what he calls the "whack-a-mole approach."

After all these marketing efforts and getting customers into your retail store and capturing them with your incredible product, enticing displays, and education, the final key is to get them coming back. To be successful, Rob warns, "You have to turn those people into repeat customers."

Yummy Yammy Salsa

Yummy Yammy of Vermont was born of owner Lisa Johnson's desire to get the nutritious so-called "super food" sweet potato into her two young daughters' diets more frequently and easily. U.S.-grown sweet potato salsa (with no tomato!) was her solution, and, as they say, the rest is history.

Lisa, who ran natural food stores for many years prior to starting Yummy Yammy, based her business on the premise that "products labeled 'food' should have nothing but food in them" and that food that is good for you can also be delicious. Her salsa has no fillers, preservatives, or chemicals.

Lisa is convinced that once people try her salsa they will be repeat customers and they will tell all their friends. To that end, while the thought of having a retail store never crossed her mind, she is often out doing demos in the stores that carry Yummy Yammy. If you are going to go to all the effort to do demos, Lisa says that you should make a point of telling people to spread the word. She also created the Yum-bassador program which gives you free shipping on your first Yummy Yammy order on Amazon.com. From there she is convinced you will be Yummy Yammy's best advocate and spread that all-important word-of-mouth advertising. Lisa also does other unique things like giving jars as prizes to trailrunners, a good target market for her healthy product.

Like many specialty food startups, Yummy Yammy started in Lisa's kitchen. Now she has a co-packer who bottles and labels, and she goes to every production run.

"It has taken me five years to find my target market," Lisa explains. When you figure out who your target market is, she says, "figure out where they are, where their conversations are taking place, and join those conversations."

Like most of the startup food businesses we talked with for this book, Lisa makes one point loud and clear: It takes a lot more money than you think to get a business like this off the ground and to the point of feeling like it is a success.

"I thought five to ten thousand dollars," she says, "and I'm going to get started, reinvest, and grow. I really believed that." She learned that you either have to realize it takes a lot of money or a long time to get beyond the startup phase. "Either plan to set aside a lot of money or find an investor right away. And don't forget, not only is it very expensive to get into the specialty food market, but you don't get paid right away; you have to make your product in advance and store it with an average of 90 days for the money on your sales [from wholesaling] to come in. In the meantime, there are a ton of expenses—things like promotions, demonstrations, and giving discounts." And if you've invented a new food, like Yummy Yammy, it especially takes time. "It takes a lot to be the first," Lisa says.

Another piece of advice Lisa has is that "it's a great time to experiment while you are small."

Winnipesaukee Chocolates

Jonathan and Sally Walpole of Wolfeboro, New Hampshire, started their chocolate business ten years ago, but it all started way before that. Jonathan's courtship of Sally included a special Valentine's Day box of chocolates that he had learned to make himself. She married him, of course, and he has been making chocolate ever since.

They moved to the Walpole family homestead and built a commercial kitchen on the property. There they make the chocolate bars that grace many retail countertops around the region. The home production center works out great. "We can take breaks when we want," Sally says, who also has a pottery studio at their home. "It really suits our lifestyle." And the day of this interview, their business had just become completely solar-powered.

"The first year," Sally says, "we researched the kind of bars we wanted to make." They chose a thick bar because it allowed for layers of chocolate with inclusions of nuts and berries that actually could be tasted in their entirety with each bite. They blend the chocolate to complement the flavors of the bars. Each chocolate base is a little different. It makes it a little more complicated, but it is just the kind of detail that puts the "specialty" in specialty food!

Just a year after starting the business, the Walpoles opened a retail storefront in downtown Wolfeboro, a resort town that has a large summer tourist influx. They thought the tourist aspect would make the store worth it but found on a day-to-day basis, people wanted to buy the more inexpensive candy bar with a local label to give as vacation gifts. And, ironically, local folks tended to look at the chocolate bars as tourist purchases. They began to feel like the retail store just took up too much time and tied them down, making it more difficult to visit children and grandchildren. They thought the retail shop would give them visibility in Wolfeboro with the skyrocketing summer population. And even though the shop has been busy during July and August and around the Christmas holiday, that just wasn't enough to make it worthwhile. Unwilling to spend their profits on employees, the Walpoles had recently decided to close the retail shop—again, a business decision based on lifestyle choices—letting other retailers sell the bars while they once again focused exclusively on production. Wholesale orders make up 80 percent of their business along with large orders for special events and mail order.

Besides the chocolate and inclusives themselves, another unique aspect of Winnipesaukee Chocolates is a beautifully designed wrapper—three of the bars show original paintings by a local artist of local lakes and mountain scenery. They wanted their business to help support the local culture all around them, so they also try to use locally sourced ingredients like honey, and for other things like the printing of the wrappers whenever possible. And if that isn't enough, Jonathan and Sally are highly conservation-minded and chose to donate a portion of their profits to local conservation groups, helping to preserve the landscape that they both love and in which they grew up.

They have lots of advice for those thinking about starting a specialty food business. But their focus of advice is related to that important time before you even make or sell that first product.

"Sit down with a business consultant and do a five-year plan," says Sally. "The first year—or even three to four years—you aren't going to make any money at it, or if you do, it will go back into the business. How will you deal with that?

"Think carefully before you get started. Make sure you think about how you really want to live your life and make sure your business fits into that quality of life. You want to have a living but you also want to have a life!"

Judy a la Carte

Judy Gilliard sells her own signature blend of spices, but after a couple halting starts at selling it to a wider market, Judy now sells it through just one specialty store. She mostly enjoys making it to give as gifts to friends and family.

Judy's life in food has included having both won and failed with restaurants and other food businesses. She has also been the guest chef on cruises, done product demos in specialty stores, and has written several books (*The Flavor Secret: Using Herbs & Spices to Put Flavor Back into Low-Fat, Low-Calorie, Low-Cholesterol Cooking* co-written with Joy Kirkpatrick, was the impetus for her spice blend) and has a longtime radio broadcasting career with a syndicated food program called Judy a la Carte. All of these experiences have given her lots of exposure to the specialty food market. Which leads Judy to reiterate the pre-startup advice that every other specialty foods producer has agreed on:

▶ Make a plan.
▶ Have funding for at least two years to support yourself while getting your business up and running.
▶ If you can't do the latter, start very very small with a limited product line.

And last, Judy feels that you need to really have a passion for the business you are starting. It's such hard work that at the end of the day, the business needs to be very meaningful to keep you motivated.

These entrepreneurs have basically been there, done that. You would do yourself a favor by listening to their advice and thinking about how their experiences starting their specialty food businesses relate to your startup plans. Here are a half dozen take-aways from these mentors that came through loud and clear:

▶ *Plan ahead before you put a single food item for sale.* And when you think you've planned enough, plan a little more.
▶ *Set aside a cash supply to carry you through the startup phase.*
▶ *Assume that startup phase will be two or three times longer* than you thought it might be.

▶ *Start a business for which you have a passion.* In this business, it is hard to keep motivated to build something if you are just doing it for money. The money is likely slow to come.

▶ *Plan your business to suit the lifestyle you would like to lead.* For example, if being stuck all day within four walls waiting around for customers to come in sounds like prison to you, don't open your own retail outlet for your product. Make your product but leave the retail sales to someone else.

▶ *Carry your personal beliefs into your business*—chemical-free foods, non-GMO ingredients, healthy choices, high-quality ingredients—and hang your toque (check the glossary!) on those beliefs. The people who share your beliefs will buy your product, and those who don't know about these things will be intrigued and impressed by your devotion.

Pass the Salt and Pepper: Business Basics

T his chapter covers much of what you will need to do before you open your doors—naming your business, determining its business structure, and finding a location. It also includes a discussion about acquiring the necessary licenses, permits, and business insurance, which are certainly not the fascinating and fun parts of your business but are critical to a solid business.

It's All in a Name

There is no question that the right name can draw your target market to you. It can also single out your specialty food business from others and keep it sharp in clients' memories. Before you decide on a name, you will need to firm up what kind of specialty food business you plan to have, the scope you want your business to have, and whether you want to convey a particular image. Will you have a highly specialized service (e.g., supplying gourmet whoopie pies to birthday parties or weddings) or a more general one (e.g., a retail outlet with catering services offering whatever specialty food strikes your fancy at the moment)? Will your range be local, national, or international? Do you want to produce only high-budget food items or do you want to cover most price ranges? Depending on your answers to these questions, a good name for your business could consist of any of the following:

tip

From smartphone apps, to iPads, to Twitter marketing, to cell phone credit-card processing, be prepared to use technology in your business. Everyone else is using it—from your customers to your suppliers to your competition—and they expect you to, as well!

▶ Description of your service (e.g., Gourmet Party Food, Inc.)
Advantages: Helps potential clients hone in on you.
Disadvantages: Creativity sometimes suffers.

▶ The type of food you specialize in (e.g., Whoop It Up!)
Advantages: Helps clients find you. You'll get fewer calls for types of foods you don't offer.
Disadvantages: Your specialization might change. What if you decide to do other kinds of baked goods or even savory items and beyond?

▶ Your name (e.g., Ann Smith, Inc.)
Advantages: People you meet while networking need remember only your name. If you use your full name, you may improve your personal credit rating as you build your business.
Disadvantages: Customers won't know what type of business this is. Worse, the IRS could confuse you and your company. And if your company goes under, your personal credit rating may suffer. Finally, if you choose to sell your business at some point, your name will become a liability. Prospective buyers prefer to buy a company that is not associated with a specific name. If Jane Doe were to buy this company and then change the name to Jane Doe, Inc., she would lose the name recognition that Ann Smith worked to build. Although you may not envision

selling your company, life has a habit of throwing some unanticipated opportunities that you might decide to take advantage of and might mean having to sell your business.

▶ Qualities your business embodies (e.g., Just Desserts)
Advantages: Helps establish the image you want to create.
Disadvantages: This kind of name pigeonholes your business. That may be okay, just be aware that if you decide in the future to include savory pies, main meals, salads, or anything that isn't desserts

tip

Make sure the name you select is not too restrictive. For instance, if you choose "Exclusively Cupcakes" you are limiting yourself to cupcakes—or to customers assuming all you do is cupcakes. Choose a name that encompasses a broader scope.

▶ The Name Game

After you've short-listed some ideas, ask yourself the following questions about each name:

▶ *Is it easy to pronounce?* People are reluctant to say a name when they're unsure of its pronunciation. This reluctance could be fatal in an industry that relies heavily on word-of-mouth advertising.

▶ *Is it short enough?* Length affects ease of pronunciation. Plus, you and your employees will have to say this name all day on the phone and still have time to do other tasks. Thus Supercalifragilisticexpialidocious, Inc. is probably not the best choice, even if you specialize in children's food items. (This name suffers from other problems, too, that probably don't need spelling out.)

▶ *Is it easy and logical to spell?* If somebody hears your company name but can't find it or call it up on the internet or spell it to a phone operator because of a unique spelling, you will lose potential clients. For this reason—and others—don't opt for a silly spelling of a common word. For instance, don't even think of a name like Kountry Kupcakes.

▶ *Is it memorable?* Despite all the above warnings, you probably want to avoid a name that sounds too ordinary. Names should be meaningful and substantive.

When you have selected a name, take the time to make sure it is not trademarked by another company. Even if you plan to keep your specialty food business small, it is a good idea to check for trademarks. You can do this for free at www.uspto.gov. Also, check popular search engines like Google and Yahoo! to see if the name you have chosen shows up on a search.

to your offerings you will have a hard time easily getting that across to potential customers.

▶ Indications of the scope of your business (e.g., Cupertino Cupcakes)
Advantages: Anyone looking under city listings will find you.
Disadvantages: Your scope might change. What if you want to branch out to other cities?

▶ A combination of the above (e.g., Ann's Desserts of Cupertino)
Advantages and disadvantages: The whole is not necessarily the sum of the parts. Consider carefully the advantages and disadvantages of each part of a combination name to see which apply.

aha!

Stop periodically and write out two lists: a "Priorities in my business life" list and an "Actual time spent" list. Compare the lists. Are you spending the greater proportion of your working life on the activities to which you give a high rank? If not, maybe it's time to reorganize.

The outline above is not an exhaustive one, but it contains some of the best ideas for creating a name that will make your business a standout in the specialty food world.

For one of this book's mentors, Susan Desjardins Burns, the name for her toffee business, Confectionately Yours, came with the business which she took on from her husband's octogenarian aunt who decided it was time to give it up herself but wanted the business to continue.

Businesses often like to select a name that will put them at the top of an alphabetical listing, but with the demise of the phone directory that is getting less and less important. AAA Gourmet Foods may position your listing in first place, but the name is not very informative. Don't sacrifice content for this prime position that may or may not be advantageous any longer.

If you buy an existing business and want to change the name (or have to, according to the sales agreement), you can take an element from the business's former name or even use the whole name.

▶ Registering Your Company Name

Most states mandate that you register your fictitious company name officially to ensure that it is unique. This is generally done through the county and is known as filing a DBA ("doing business as") statement. If the name you chose is already being used, you will be asked to choose something else. For this reason, it's a good idea to have a backup name or two. There is typically a nominal ($30 to $60) cost for this service.

A good name is well worth the effort you'll put into finding it. With some thought, you can end up with a name as unique as your business. Use the worksheet in Figure 4–1 to help you craft your business name.

Business Name Worksheet

List three (or more) variations using your own name for your business:

1. _____

2. _____

3. _____

List three business name ideas associated with your specialty or niche as a purveyor of specialty food:

1. _____

2. _____

3. _____

List three business name ideas associated with your geographic area. You can use the name of your town, county, or state. Or use something that your area is well known for, such as a southwestern region or pristine beaches.

1. _____

2. _____

3. _____

Once you've narrowed it down to one or two choices, take the following steps:

▶ Write it down to see how it looks.

▶ Say it out loud to hear how it sounds.

▶ Check the first initials of each word to make sure the acronym isn't something inappropriate.

▶ Run it by family and friends to see if they are as enthusiastic as you are.

▶ Look in the Yellow Pages and on the web to see if someone else is using it.

▶ Call the county clerk or secretary of state's office to make arrangements for filing it.

FIGURE 4–1: **Business Name Worksheet**

On a Mission

Your mission statement should be more than a sentence or two about what you do—it should serve as a framework and reminder of your specific goals and help keep you on track while making decisions down the road. Those decisions might seem confusing, but if you can look at your mission and put them in that context, then your mission statement will be doing the job it's intended to do.

That's why constructing your mission statement should come from your heart and soul. It should reflect why you wanted to start your business in the first place, the key thing you want to spend most of your time on. It should leave no doubt in anyone's mind what kind of business you are.

Your mission statement should not just serve you and your business but should appeal to the range of customer types you intend to serve as well as any potential investors in startup or expansion funding. It should get across your enthusiasm and intent. See Figure 4–2 on page 43 for a worksheet to help you develop your mission statement.

Here are a couple mission statements from specialty food purveyors:

▶ *DPI Specialty Foods* (http://dpispecialtyfoods.com): "DPI's mission is to provide all customers with an extensive variety of specialty foods from around the world, including Gourmet, Natural, Organic, Gluten-Free, Local and Ethnic foods."

▶ *Omaha Steaks* (www.omahasteaks.com): "We deliver exceptional experiences that bring people together. Guaranteed."

After you have written your mission statement, put it on probation. Ask customers if they feel it expresses what they were looking for when they found you and if what they got was what the mission statement says. When you are sure it's right, put it on your website and in marketing materials. If you have a retail store, post it where customers will see it and post it where employees will constantly be able to read it and be reminded of why you are doing what you do.

warning

Having office space in your retail shop is very convenient and probably a good idea. However, do not get involved in office work while you are the only one in the shop. Your office work will suffer from the (hopefully) regular interruptions, and customers do not like to walk into an unattended space where they have to seek you out in the back room to help them. Most will walk out instead.

Choosing a Business Location

The type of specialty food business you plan to start as well as the size of your business are among the factors that

Mission Statement Worksheet

To develop an effective mission statement, answer these questions:

1. What products and/or services do we produce or offer?

   _____

   _____

2. In what geographic location do we operate?

   _____

   _____

3. Why does our company exist? Whom do we serve? What is our purpose?

   _____

   _____

4. What are our strengths, weaknesses, opportunities, and threats?

   _____

   _____

   _____

   _____

5. Considering the above, along with our expertise and resources, what business should we be in?

   _____

   _____

6. What is important to us? What do we stand for?

   _____

   _____

FIGURE 4–2: **Mission Statement Worksheet**

▶ Office Location Pointers

The type of specialty food business you are starting will have a lot of bearing on your office location:

- ▶ If you are opening a retail shop, you will want to be sure your shop has some space for a small office. You can plan a half hour before and/or after opening to keep office work up-to-date.

- ▶ If your specialty food business is more of a wholesale operation, carving out an office in your wholesale space is a good idea. Then, assuming you have employees, you can be making client calls and lining up deliveries, but if questions arise you are there.

- ▶ Having a home office space is logical if you are not the one who is doing the day-to-day business of your business. That is, if others are doing the baking or cooking or bottling or staffing the retail storefront, then you can work remotely and it probably doesn't matter. However, few startup businesses have the luxury of the owner being that hands-off.

will determine where you set up shop. Your location can be anywhere from your home, in a retail space, or in a commercial warehouse-type location.

If you're starting small, a homebased specialty food business may be the ideal choice for you. This option keeps overhead low and saves travel time to and from the office. One potential problem is that friends and family might drop in at all hours because you're "not really working." Be firm. Set up business hours and stick to them.

Business Types

Congratulations! You have named your business, have your DBA in hand, and you are considered the owner of a legitimate business. Now you will need to make the decision to operate as one of four business entities: a sole proprietorship, a partnership, a limited liability company (LLC), or a corporation.

aha!

Consider sharing space with a related business. For example, you could set up shop with a noncompeting type of gourmet food—and if you each do your own catering, you can still operate as distinct businesses. You might not only save money but also gain referrals. If you elect to share space, however, make sure you have a clear contract stating how space and responsibilities will be shared. Also, be sure to share space with a well-respected business—your reputation will be mixed with theirs, good or bad!

▶ Separating Home and Business

If you opt for a homebased business, you need to allocate a space that is to be used solely for your business. It could be a small area, a desk tucked into the corner of the dining room, for instance, but it must be devoted to your specialty food business. It is also wise to have separate phone lines for your home and for your business. Chances are your main business phone will be a cell phone anyway. However, nothing will kill your credibility faster than using your home phone line with its answering machine featuring your three-year-old singing the theme song from *Frozen*. While cute, this is not professional.

Keeping home and business as separate as possible, especially when they are in the same building, will also help when tax time rolls around since your business phone expenses will be deductible.

Sole Proprietor

Sole proprietor is the easiest type of business to form. All you have to do is file a DBA, as already discussed, then open a business checking account in that name. You can use your personal credit card to pay for business expenditures, yet you still get tax benefits like business expense deductions.

While it is easy, there is a downside to the sole proprietorship. You are personally liable for any losses, bankruptcy claims, legal actions, and so on. That can wipe out both your personal and business assets if major problems arise.

General Partnership

Perhaps you are planning to work with someone else to form your business. Then you are forming a general partnership. While a little more complicated to form than sole proprietorships, they are easier than corporations. You don't have to file any documents to make them legal but you do want a crystal clear partnership agreement stating what each partner is responsible for.

Limited Liability Company

A third type of business entity is the limited liability company, or LLC, which has the tax structure of a partnership, yet protects the business owner from personal

warning

Never put a client on hold to speak with another client. Let your voice mail pick up any incoming calls you can't answer yourself.

liability. This structure protects each partner's personal interests.

Corporations

The last type of business arrangement is the corporation. It is established as a totally separate legal entity from the business owner. Establishing a corporation requires filing articles of incorporation, electing officers, and holding an annual meeting. Very small businesses do not usually choose this route initially because the costs are prohibitive and the company must pay corporate taxes. On the other hand, a corporation will find it easier to obtain financing, which would be useful if you decided to franchise your business or expand in a big way.

Although the process for creating a corporate structure is more complicated and expensive than other structures, it does offer protection to business owners and their assets. It alone is legally responsible for its actions and debts. As an employee of the corporation, your personal assets are protected in most situations, even though you may own all or most of the stock.

If deciding on a legal form for your business keeps you up at night, consider this: Your business structure is not carved in stone. It can be changed.

Licenses and Permits

Most cities and counties require business operators to obtain various licenses and permits to comply with local regulations. For everyday operation of a food business, you may need the following:

- ▶ *Business license*: ensures proper zoning and parking
- ▶ *Vendor's permit* (varies from state to state): allows you to buy and resell
- ▶ Health department permit: if you handle food

tip

To find out if you need additional licenses or permits, check these sources:

- ▶ Small Business Administration, www.sba.gov
- ▶ Small Business Development Center, www.sba.gov
- ▶ Service Corps of Retired Executives, www.score.org

And always talk with the municipality in which you do business.

tip

Some cities provide packets with explanations and all the forms you'll need for the various licenses and permits, so investigate this possibility at your town clerk's office. Also, it's a good idea to ask more than one city or county employee about the licenses you need, especially if you get information that is confusing or not what you expected.

▶ *Liquor, wine, and beer licenses*: if you yourself serve alcohol

▶ *Sign permit*: covers size, location, and sometimes the type of sign you may use

▶ *County permits*: may be applicable if you are located outside city limits

Check local regulations to see which of the above licenses and permits you'll need or if there are others depending on what you plan to do in your business, like actually host rather than just cater events.

warning

Be aware that distinctive trademarks are protected. For example, you may need permission to use any relevant brand names on literature you circulate about your business.

Choosing Insurance

Knowing what kind of insurance to carry and how much to obtain is an important aspect of good risk management. Don't view insurance as an option. It is absolutely imperative for any business to have the appropriate insurance.

As the owner of a specialty food business, you are most likely to need the following types of insurance:

▶ *General liability insurance.* This is the one type of insurance you must carry. General liability insurance protects a business against accidents and injuries that might occur at your office or retail site.

▶ *Workers' compensation insurance.* If you have employees, you will also want this type of insurance. You are liable for injury to employees at work caused by problems with equipment or working conditions. In every state, an employer must insure against potential workers' comp claims. However, employee coverage and the extent of the employer's liability vary among states.

▶ *Auto insurance.* Cars and trucks are sources of liability. Even if your business does not own a vehicle, you can be liable for injuries and property damage caused by employees operating their own or someone else's car while on company business.

warning

If you operate your business from your home, you may need additional coverage. Your homeowner's policy may be sufficient, but if you plan to store or use expensive machinery, such as a computer, or if customers or clients will visit your home for business purposes, you may want to purchase additional coverage. Set up an appointment with your agent to go over your overall insurance coverage.

► *Food-specific insurance.* Don't leave out this important ingredient! Look for an insurance company that knows the specific needs of a food and/or beverage manufacturer or retailer.

► *Bonding.* This is pertinent particularly if part of your business includes catering. You may need bonding to protect you if one of your employees steals or damages something at an event site. Vendors should carry their own protection. Check your state's legal requirements.

Forms

To do business (and protect your company as you do it), you'll need a variety of documents. Invoices and purchase orders are standard fare for any business. However, if you plan to do special orders and events or catering, you will want specific kinds of forms.

Proposals

Proposals simply tell clients what you will do for them and at what cost. It is an important selling tool and might consist of any or all of the following elements:

► *History of your company.* Provide one if relevant.

► *Letters of reference.* Kudos from clients for whom you done similar work.

► *Write-ups.* A complimentary newspaper or magazine article featuring your business is often a valuable tool for selling your services to others. You may also want to include photographs.

► *Description of services.* This tells exactly how you will achieve what your client is asking from your business.

► *Listing of additional services.* If you also will provide floral design, specialty dishware, or some other service, describe those services completely. Does the dishware belong to the client after? If it is supposed to come back to you, how will it get there?

► *Cost estimate.* This accompanies any proposal.

tip

We've all heard it: A picture is worth a thousand words. Photos in your proposal packet can make a powerful impact on prospective clients. Consider hiring a professional photographer to capture some stellar images for you; at the very least, invest in a high-quality digital camera. Even though phone cameras are now quite high quality, don't rely on images from your camera to use to market your business in print advertising and brochures.

▶ *Term of validity.* Make sure you include in your proposal an expiration date for the estimate. You don't want to be expected to follow through on that proposal five years from now for the listed price for five years ago!

Customers must be able to visualize your offering and understand the quality of your work when they read your proposal. Consider including in your proposal some photos of your product that is similar to what the client wants.

tip

Quotes from satisfied customers, called "testimonials," are great to include in marketing pieces, proposals, and ads. They are more convincing if they include a real name (or first name, last initial); just be sure to get the customer's permission.

Agreements

Lots of specialty food businesses include event catering in their list of offerings. A signed document detailing all aspects of the expectations of your participation is not only helpful but also imperative to the legal health of your business. Are you to provide dishware, utensils, napkins, chafing dishes? You likely want to be the one setting your food up to be sure it is being presented as you intended, so include that in the agreement.

Invoices

While a mainly retail business setup likely won't hand out many invoices, you will want to have a standard invoice on hand even if you only do a handful of large orders a year. You can also use invoices to show donations that you can keep copies of for your tax records. It's always good to have written money records. Create a custom invoice on your computer in a "basic forms" folder. There is no longer a need to have invoices printed out unless you want to buy a preprinted stack at the office supply store and have a custom stamp created that you can use to customize the form.

warning

If you are going to take the time to do a written agreement for services like catering (and you should!), be sure to cover the details. For example, you might want to include a check box that gives you permission to take photographs of the food you prepare for an event and use them in your marketing materials if you desire. Most people would be flattered, but it's always best to ask.

Receipts

Again, you may not use a lot of receipts if you are a cash-based retail-focused business, but if you do those special event large orders or even smaller orders for individuals—

▶ Foundation Checklist

Complete these items as you get your business started:

- ▶ Develop and write a business plan
- ▶ Create a powerful mission statement
- ▶ Select a name for your company and apply for a DBA
- ▶ Choose the best business structure for your company
- ▶ Check local zoning laws to ensure that you are in compliance
- ▶ Apply for the licenses and permits you will need

like other business owners who are purchasing your product for business-related gifts—they will want a receipt to be able to use for tax purposes.

You've Been Chopped!: Market Research

O nce you have determined to pursue your dream in the specialty food business, you will need to get a handle on where your business will fit in. First you will research the global picture of your specialty type and then you will want to drill down into your niche in the marketplace in your location. Whatever you do, research as much as you can so you don't, as the popular foodie TV show forewarns, get chopped!

Industry Research

You know you want to take your whoopie pie recipe to the next level beyond your friends and family telling you they are the best or most creative whoopie pies they have ever seen. You could certainly just start making them and selling them, and perhaps you have. But if you want to make a living at your dream or want to create a whoopie pie empire that you might be able to sell down the road when you are ready to move on, you need to start your empire with a bit more planning.

What you have decided on for a business model will dictate what market you need to research. Figuring out the best place to site your retail shop will require very different research than if you plan to start a mail order business.

The Specialty Food Business

Your first market research will be about the specialty food business in general. This isn't intended to tell you whether or not you want to enter the business—that ship has likely already sailed. But you do want to know about the industry you are getting into and you want to include some of that information in your business plan. If you use your business plan to get financing, which most small businesses do, you will want not only to inform them about the state of the industry, but to show your potential investors that you are informed.

The Specialty Food Association

First off, join. The Specialty Food Association offers a "membership candidate" category for a $100 application fee intended to "help new manufacturers gain the knowledge and experience they need to grow in the marketplace, and transition to full membership." It includes mentoring, one free 30-minute consultation with SFA's legal or trademark advisor, and other benefits intended to get you off the ground to a successful specialty food business.

But even if you don't join, you can browse certain parts of their website and glean important information. Articles such as "The State of the Specialty Food Industry 2015" and "Small Food Companies Gain Ground on Big Brands" can give you valuable insight into the industry you are about to join.

State of the Industry

And what about the "The State of the Specialty Food Industry 2015"? The article says:

- ► Sales of specialty food in the U.S. topped $100 billion for the first time in 2014.
- ► That said, the market's growth has slowed slightly.
- ► Specialty food stores captured a 10.6 percent share of the overall specialty food market.
- ► The top ten specialty food categories were: 1) cheese; 2) coffee; 3) frozen meats and seafood; 4) chips, pretzels, snacks; 5) bread/baked goods; 6) candy; 7) condiments; 8) frozen entrees; 9) yogurt; 10) nuts, seeds, dried fruits, and veggies, in that order.
- ► The three fastest growing categories were refrigerated pasta, eggs, and refrigerated pasta and pizza sauces.

The report also found the following emerging trends:

- ► Local, sustainable, whole grains, humane food production
- ► Smoked flavors, healthy food, pickled everything
- ► More gluten-free, use of beets, kale, seaweed, coconut, and other good-for-you ingredients
- ► Return to simple, clean, and old-fashioned, e.g., real grass butter, fermented foods, ancient grains
- ► Smaller stores, more specialty grass-fed products, home gardening, far greater delivery options

Packaging

The food itself isn't the only part of the specialty food market you to which you will want to pay attention. Packaging is a huge part of the industry; sometimes packaging alone can help launch a food product to success. The packaging can be unique, like Phoenix Wrappers' stretch wrapping intended to allow perishable food products to breathe. This unique system slices "stretch film during the wrapping process to create gaps in the wrap so that food can 'breathe,'" eliminating the need for specialty film that has breathable holes in it and is expensive (www.FoodProductiondaily.com, "Kellogg's Stretch Wrapper Provider Launches Breathable Wrap for Perishable Food," by Jenny Eagle, 9/11/15).

"New packaging can redefine a category," says Blake Mitchell in "The IKEA Effect: There Is a Total Respect for Design That Now Goes Well Beyond Furniture and Gadgets" (http://foodnavigator-usa.com). He points to IKEA, Target, and Apple as setting the bar for other industries to get on board with creative packaging and attention to package design.

Pointing to nut butters that started making their product in squeeze packs that can be eaten on the go, the design actually created a new category of specialty food.

You don't have to have a unique product to come up with unusual packaging. In fact, a common product in unique packaging would be more attention-getting—like "boxed wine" and now starting to make an appearance, "boxed water." Whatever you do, however, don't create unique packaging that doesn't work well or you will get the opposite kind of attention to the kind you want.

Also keep in mind that unique packaging definitely needs to have the potential for bringing in higher sales since anything that is too original likely will require original production equipment. Also consider how it will play on the shelf—will those carrying your product need a special display rack? Will it topple over easily if placed on a normal shelf? Should it be hung?

The bottom line is, think about your product and its packaging. While you probably shouldn't break the bank on packaging, could it be a value-added enhancement to call attention to what you know is a delicious and healthy food?

Packaging Market Research

Packaging is a fascinating study in itself. You have targeted your market as 30-somethings who care about what they put in their bodies. If they care about nutrition and GMO-free or organic foods, they also likely care about the environment. How do you think they would feel about loving your product only to have it come in the mail shrink-wrapped in a cardboard box inside a Styrofoam container and shrink-wrapped again? You would likely lose them as a customer after the first purchase and they would tell their friends not to purchase from you either.

Take the Clif Bar Company as an example. They promote a line of "all-natural and organic energy and nutrition food and drinks." Their famous Clif Bar energy bars come wrapped in brown paper wrappers with a simple yet colorful rock-climbing illustration. Their website has an "impact" button that talks about their attempt to lower their ecological footprint and help build healthier, more sustainable communities. This packaging is definitely in keeping with their target market's belief system.

And speaking of that rock-climbing image, it's not just the packaging material but the design that matters.

stat fact

"Local" and "organic" are the trends today. Specialty Food Association report "The State of the Specialty Food Industry 2015" indicates that in three years those trends will be "local," "sustainable," and "non-GMO."

Retail Market Research

Probably the best market research you can do for your retail specialty food business is boots-on-the-ground research in your own market area. If you haven't yet decided where you plan to set up shop, you will want to do market research in several different areas to help make your decision. Assuming you don't plan to locate your retail food store more than 10 or 20 miles from your home, this should be an easy enough task.

There are two approaches you will want to take:

1. Look at retail stores of all types in the areas you are considering locating your shop.
2. Analyze the specialty-food-specific shops in the region.

Bring a notebook. Be sure to not only take notes but to jot down a general list of categories and questions so that you are comparing and considering each location under the same microscope.

The Research

In your research of the overall retail market in your targeted area (or areas, if you have not decided on a location), look at:

▶ What is the demographic of the population?
▶ Are shoppers in that area local or are they coming in from a distance?
▶ What types of retail shops are there? Thrift shops, dollar stores, pop-up seasonal stores, small take-out restaurants, and chain drugstores? Or high-end clothing shops, jewelry stores, sit-down dining, and specialty stores like photo shops and chocolatiers?
▶ What is the price-point range of the merchandise? Do the stores tend to have sidewalk sale racks or discounted sections up front in the store? Or are the display windows done in high-style displays changed on regular basis, with the marked-down clothing on a rack at the very back of the store?
▶ Do the shoppers come away with merchandise in custom rope-handled shopping bags or in used plastic bags from the grocery store?

---

fun fact

"Specialty foods are defined as foods or beverages of the highest grade, style, and/or quality in their respective categories. Their specialty nature derives from a combination of some or all of the following qualities: uniqueness, origin, processing method, design, limited supply, unusual application or use, extraordinary packaging, or channel of distribution/sales."

—Specialty Food Association, "The State of the Specialty Food Industry" (www.specialtyfood.com)

► Are shoppers actually coming out of the stores having purchased merchandise?

► What kind of staffing do the shops have? Are they mostly one-person shops where the owner is also the cashier and sits behind the counter eating her bagged lunch? Or do the shops tend to have someone at the cash register, another person helping customers on the floor, and the owner out in the back ready to help with questions but in the meantime ordering and doing bookkeeping and other back-office tasks?

Determining Store Size

One metric used in the retail industry is to determine your sales per square foot of floor space. Typically it is used after the fact to figure out how much your business is bringing in per square foot. So if you average $1,000 per day out of a 200-square-foot store, you are making $50 per square foot per day.

aha!

The seasonal storefront known as a "pop-up store" is becoming popular. Open storefronts that are between leases rent on a short-term basis around Halloween, Christmas, or Mother's Day. If your product is one that would be popular during one of these time frames, a pop-up store might be a great way to make some extra money and expose your product to a wider audience.

This kind of calculation can also help you determine how big of a space you need. If you want to sell $2,000 per day of product, you need to have a store big enough to hold the product. Many factors come into play here, of course. They include:

► *The size of your product.* If you have small jars of jam that stack neatly into square shelving units built into the walls, you can pack a lot of product into a smaller space than if you are selling puffy bags of specialty potato chips.

► *The retail price of your product.* If your jams are selling at $7.50 per jar, you will need to sell 267 jars a day for gross sales of $2,000. On the other hand, you would need to sell 404 bags of $4.95/bag potato chips to get to the $2,000. Your space would actually need to be larger to accommodate the potato chips!

► *Other products.* Perhaps your key product, the one that got you into the specialty foods business, isn't the only thing you sell in the store. If you have gourmet nacho chips, maybe a local potter can sell nacho plates in your store. This would help dress up your store and if you sell them on consignment you don't have to put out any money on inventory. But it would take up more space . . .

► *Special display needs.* Does your product have a unique size or shape that requires special display for potential customers to be able to see the product in its best light?

If yours is a product that is a great gift item, customers will want to see exactly what the gift recipient will see when he or she opens the package. You may want space in your shop to display a sample of the packaged item.

▶ *Nonsales floor space.* What kind of space do you need that isn't specifically selling space? Obviously your cash-out counter is one such area, although that can be offset with impulse items like a rack of wine bottle necklaces or oven mitts for those nachos. Do you need bathrooms accessible to customers? Space for staff breaks? An office area with space for a computer for bookkeeping and marketing? Space for packaging and mailing? Will you be doing production here as well? That will be a huge consideration.

All of these should be taken into account to determine the best space for your retail store. Figuring them out in advance as much as possible will help you quickly weed out, and not be tempted by, spaces that just don't make the cut.

warning

Retail is not for everyone. "It didn't even occur to me," says Lisa Johnson of Yummy Yammy of running a retail store as part of her salsa business. The idea of sitting around waiting for people to come into her store and buy her product just didn't seem like a good use of her time, nor did staffing a store seem like a good use of resources. It may be different for you, but you may want to try it out with a part-time job in an existing store before going into retail yourself.

stat fact

Pop-up stores allow you to test your idea before you take it bigger, according to an article by Alexandra Powers called "The Power of the Pop-Up Business" (www.cnbc.com, 8/21/15). And according to the article, consumers love pop-up stores as well for the uniqueness of the experience. Lawyer Jessica Tucker launched a pop-up festival in the U.K. called Urban Food Fest—every Saturday 15 food trucks appear with a new themed selection of cocktails, food, and musicians.

Production Space

Whether you are going to set up as a retail space with a production area in the back or just a production space and use retailers, distributors, and/or mail order through which to sell your product, the production area of your specialty food business is perhaps the most critical. The main market research you need to do in this regard is whether the production of your product will have any impact on the market and how you are perceived.

Special Diets

A gluten-free product may, for instance, have production marketing implications especially if you sell other non-gluten-free products. Do you need to have each made in different areas? Can you clean instruments, utensils, bakeware, and production surfaces well enough to make the gluten-free products in the same area that products with gluten ingredients are made? And even if you can, will your market believe it is sufficient that you say you clean the surfaces well?

Your reliability in the market of gluten-free products or whatever your specialty—nut-free, organic foods—may be influenced by this decision. You don't want to set up in too small a space only to find you didn't address this properly. And check out what your competitors do; that will tell you a lot.

warning

Specialty food businesses say three of the biggest threats to their businesses are "deep discounting by competitors," "high cost of distributor networks," and "capital and cash-flow management."

—Specialty Food Association, "The State of the Specialty Food Industry 2015"

Retail/Production Combo

Are you able to locate in a building/area that allows you to have both a storefront as well as a production area? Some segments of the specialty market, like craft beer and small wineries, have made it a selling point to have their production not only visible but capable of providing an interesting and educational tour for customers. Taffy shops on the beach often have their taffy-making equipment in the window for passersby to watch the taffy being made and entice them to come in and make a purchase—and tell others about how cool the process is.

If production is the part of the process you are focused on and decide to leave the retailing to someone else, don't be lured into a space with a storefront that doesn't quite meet your production needs. Again, research how your competitors do it. Ask around if producers in other categories find the combo a worthwhile venture.

Mail Order

Often the production-focused facility also uses mail/online ordering as a prime selling vehicle—if this is what your market expects, you will want to include shipping preparation as part of your facility. You do not want to be packing things up to move them somewhere else to get them on their way to the purchaser.

save

One way to save but still do a professional focus group is to hire a marketing class at a local business school to conduct one for you. Check with a marketing professor about when focus groups come up in the class. The school might even have a room with a one-way mirror designed to do focus groups.

Focus Groups

Don't try to figure out all this for yourself. If you can afford a company to put together a focus group for you, that is great. At the very least, conduct your own focus group with friends and friends of friends or even strangers that you solicit through, say, the local yoga center or the men's basketball team and ask them to do an informal focus group for your product for pizza and some free product. Ask them the questions you have in mind and give them free rein to tell you what comes to their minds as they look at and taste your product. The most important thing is to listen to what they have to say. While the focus group consultants will know how to conduct focus groups with the most value, you can still gain a lot out of conducting one yourself.

What Makes You Stand Out?

The result of all your market research should ultimately help you answer the question: What makes your product/business stand out? What gives you a competitive edge over those you consider to be in your market?

You don't have to go way out on a limb to stand out with some whacky logo or product. Whoopie pies with meat-flavored frosting or that are packaged with a singing elf will make you stand out, but not necessarily in a good way. And not necessarily in a way that will make the expense pay for itself.

But you do need to have a product that is somehow different from all the rest. Yummy Yammy salsa stands out, for example, for its main ingredient being sweet potatoes. Newman's Own products stand out because the company puts Paul Newman's face on the labels and has done a great job making it

tip

Watch what the big kids do and think about how it may impact your business. For example, Nestlé recently announced plans to remove artificial flavors and lower sodium levels in its frozen pizzas. According to the market research firm Mintel, "Any move that Nestlé makes across its huge pizza portfolio is likely to have residual effects for the whole category." ("Nestlé slashes salt from frozen pizzas, but there's no algae substitute . . . yet" by Alex Beckett, 9/4/15)

well known that the company uses organic ingredients and donates its profits to charity. When Susan Desjardins Burns took over her husband's 80-year-old aunt's toffee recipe, she updated it making one significant change reflecting contemporary food choices: she substituted the high fructose corn syrup with agave nectar.

These are competitive edges that make the consumer purchase one product over another.

6

The Necessary Ingredient: Financing

Your funding needs will of course depend on the type of food business you are planning to start. A small specialty jam business that you conduct from your home and sell only to friends by personal sales is going to take a lot less startup funding than a bakery that makes and sells specialty whoopie pies to the public and events like weddings and anniversaries or a retail gourmet food store in an upscale part of Main Street that will require rent, deposits, utilities, lease-hold improvements, special display racking, and a couple of employees, etc.

First Things First

The first step is to estimate your business expenditures over the startup period (for some that may be longer than others, both because of the type of business and also personal circumstances) and over the first six months of operation. Once you have your costs put them into the "Startup Expenses Worksheet," Figure 6–1. If you haven't estimated those costs yet, now is a good time to do so.

The basic startup costs are for expenses you will incur whether you sell a single food item or not—these

save

For good deals on office furniture check www. officefurniture2go.com. They offer competitive shipping and prices. There really is no need to buy new for your startup office.

are "fixed costs" for the most part. Many specialty food businesses will need to add a line or more about the cost of ingredients. If you have a retail outlet, you will need to have food on the shelves for sale. If you do only event catering, you will at least need to include the costs of ingredients for creating food for tasting until you get a deposit for your first event. For example, if your specialty food business is gourmet cupcakes that are decorated to look like a bouquet of flowers, you will need to create some bouquets to wow customers and you will need to have fresh cupcakes at the ready for potential customers to sample. All of this costs money.

Don't Forget Life

These startup costs need to include the money you require for the business as well as what you personally need for your own living expenses until your business makes a profit. If you are starting your business part time while you finish up a career in a different field, this will impact how much startup funding you will need.

Perhaps you are recently retired and have been planning and saving for your startup foodie business for a decade. This won't lessen the amount you need for fixed costs for your business but it will greatly impact how much funding you need from outside sources to get started. If you saved enough to cover your own living expenses while you get your business up and running (good for you!), your startup funding needs will only be what is directly related to the business.

Startup Expenses Worksheet

Item	Estimated Cost
Mortgage/rent	
Office equipment, furniture, supplies	
Business licenses/permits	
Phone (landline)	
Phone (cell phone)	
Owner/operator salary	
Employee wages and benefits (first six months)	
Startup advertising/marketing	
Accounting/legal services	
Insurance (annual cost)	
Membership dues (annual)	
Publications (annual subscriptions)	
Online services (broadband)	
Website design	
Web hosting, domain name (annual cost)	
Subtotal	
Miscellaneous expenses (roughly 10% of total)	
Total	

FIGURE 6–1: **Startup Expenses Worksheet**

Finding Financing

Your best source of financing is you. Not only should you invest your own resources first, anyone you approach for funding will expect you to. Perhaps you are fortunate to be able to sell another business and use the proceeds toward your specialty food startup.

Here are potential sources to add to your startup pot:

▶ *Friends and family.* Use extreme care when exercising this option. You could very easily sour a lifelong friendship or make family gatherings very uncomfortable. Even if you are getting funding from a family member or friend, be sure to create a written contract even if you write it yourself, but it wouldn't hurt to enlist an attorney. The contract should stipulate your obligations as well as the agreement of the transaction. Is this a loan? A gift? Is there a deadline by which the lender needs the money back? Will the lender receive interest? Percentage of profits? Spell out every deal and make sure you both understand and agree on the transaction completely.

▶ *Credit cards.* This is a financing option that should also be used with caution. Interest on credit cards can become crippling and could easily steal your profits. Be especially careful with cards with low initial rates—know exactly when those rates go up and make note of when you need to pay the startup financing before the initial period ends and the higher rate kicks in. Likewise with 0 percent cards—often the interest, when it kicks in, is much higher than average, so if you aren't certain you can pay that debt off before the interest starts, find another option. Sometimes the interest even kicks back to the original amount of the loan even if you have paid a portion of it.

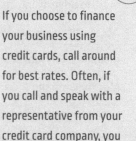

tip

If you choose to finance your business using credit cards, call around for best rates. Often, if you call and speak with a representative from your credit card company, you can negotiate a better rate than the one advertised.

▶ *Equity.* Home equity is certainly an option but again, one to be considered carefully. While it can wisely utilize your investment in your home, remember—you are utilizing your investment in your home. You still need to pay interest on the loan and you need to be sure to leave enough equity available to you for a large unexpected home repair. The last thing you need is to compromise what is often a homeowner's most significant asset.

▶ *Venture capital.* Venture capitalists are private lenders. They tend to invest in high-risk businesses that have potential for huge returns if successful. Few specialty food startup businesses will be able to gain the attention of venture capitalists.

▶ **Crowdfunding Sites to Check Out**

> ▶ www.Kickstarter.com: creative projects

> ▶ www.Indiegogo.com: creative, personal, hobbyist

> ▶ www.Crowdfunder.com: investment raising

> ▶ www.RocketHub.com: creative with campaign guidance

> ▶ www.Appbackr.com: mobile apps

▶ *Banks.* Your good old basic bank will likely be the most fruitful place to go for business funding. For this typically conservative, more traditional source of funding, you will need a thoughtful and detailed business plan. Local banks will be more interested in financing local businesses. Don't bring your pie-in-the-sky ideas; save those for down the road when your fundamental business is up and running and a proven good investment.

▶ *Small Business Administration.* Contact the SBA (www.sba.gov) for information about financing your startup business. They often work through local banks and can help you secure lending.

▶ *Crowdfunding.* Whether crowdfunding is a potential funding source for your business will depend on the type of specialty food business you are planning. Many crowdfunding sources do best with a product that you can promise to send people in exchange for their investment. See the sidebar above for a list of several crowdfunding sites and explore a few to figure out how others set up their pitch.

Being wise with your capital needs and heading into financing with a thorough business plan is the best advice for a new entrepreneur.

Get Your Credit in Shape

You will want to establish two different credit profiles: personal and business. Before you have business credit, you will have a personal credit profile. This should be as rosy as you can possibly make it. A key to having a good personal credit profile is to get rid of debt if you have it. Clark Howard, at his website subtitled "Money in Your Pocket," offers five steps for getting out of debt:

1. Make a conscious decision to stop borrowing money.

2. Establish a starter Emergency Fund of $1,000. You need something for emergencies instead of using credit cards (see number 1).

3. Create a realistic budget and stick to it. Cut a few things like gym memberships you pay regularly but rarely utilize, cut dining out in half, make coffee at home instead of stopping at the café.

4. Organize your debt. Decide whether to pay off high-interest debt first (called "laddering") or whether you want to tackle debt from the lowest amount owed on up which can give you a boost toward your goal as you see a debt paid off.

5. Throw any excess cash at your debt.

Come to think of it, these aren't bad suggestions for business debt, too. If you want to read more about these five steps, go to the website at www.clarkhoward.com/paying-off-credit-card-debt.

Networking

Networking is more than a buzzword—it will help you with all aspects of your business, including funding. In addition to tapping your network as you formulate your business, work toward expanding your network. Attend chamber of commerce functions in your market area, go to conferences, seminars, and trade shows to expand your network, and most of all, reach out to your friends, former colleagues, and other acquaintances; let them know you are starting a business, and ask them to let their friends and acquaintances know.

Your Business Plan

We could have discussed business plans in Chapter 4, since business plans are part of the salt-and-pepper basics of any startup. But business plans usually come into practical use when you are trying to obtain financing, so we'll talk about creating one here in the money chapter.

Your business plan should include a broad discussion of the specialty food industry, particularly as it pertains

tip

There are five things an entrepreneur should be prepared to show a loan officer:

1. A business plan showing how you will use the financing

2. Proof that you pay your obligations when due

3. Proof that you have enough equity to cover the obligation

4. That your team has enough experience to implement your plan

5. That your sales prospects are strong enough to repay the loan

to your specific part of the industry—i.e., retail, service, events. Also include information about your business structure, your clients, the competition and how you will fit into it, your income, cash flow, and expenses, and other relevant financial information. This is the chief instrument you will use to communicate your ideas to others—not only bankers but other business people and potential partners. And the business plan will become the basis for any loan proposal.

stat fact

Fifty-two percent of all small businesses are homebased, according to SCORE's Small Biz Stats & Trends (www.score.org/node/148155).

A relevant business plan will help you gauge your progress in starting and building your business. Use it as an operating tool to help you manage your business. The plan will help you cement the logistics and growth curve of your new business. And don't be afraid to veer from your plan if it makes sense—you need to have a plan to begin with in order to veer from it.

The Components of a Successful Business Plan

Every thorough and useful business plan should contain the following seven components:

1. *Executive summary*. As the name suggests, this section summarizes your entire business plan. It includes details about the nature of your business, the type and scope of services that you will provide, the legal form of your business (covered in Chapter 4), and your vision and goals for the business.

2. *Business description*. In this section you'll describe the gourmet and specialty food business as a whole and your chosen target market. Use specifics here, hard numbers, and facts. Along with those found throughout this book, you'll find more business statistics at websites like www.census.gov, www.statista.com, and www.dol.gov (Department of Labor).

3. *Market strategies*. Here you will describe exactly how you will reach out to and market to prospective clients. Again, be as specific as possible. Will you advertise in the Yellow Pages? Join professional organizations for networking? Create a website? Use newsletters as a marketing device? Social media? Include as many of these details as possible. Also, take time in this section to write about the ways in which your company is unique and, therefore, better than your competitors.

4. *Competitive analysis*. In this section, focus on likely competitors in your field. Discuss how your business will differ from other specialty food businesses in your market area. Also, don't forget to focus on other potential competitors, such as

gourmet sections of high-end grocery stores or restaurants providing gourmet and specialty food catering services. Why are your services preferable to those of your competitors? It is essential that you clearly formulate the ways in which your company will differentiate itself from competitors. This will require a little boots-on-the-ground research.

5. *Design and development plan.* This is an opportunity to discuss how you will develop markets for your business and develop an ever-broadening client base. Set specific goals. Perhaps you plan to cater to 12 events during your first year of business and to grow that number to 50 events per year by your fifth year in the specialty food business. Or maybe you plan to eventually host classes at your retail site or rent your commercial kitchen space out to other specialty food businesses.

6. *Operations and management plan.* How will you run your business on a day-to-day basis? Will this be a part- or full-time career for you? Will you hire employees? Consider a typical day in your business and describe it here and how you will facilitate this operation.

7. *Financial factors.* This is the section in which to focus on your financial expectations. Even if you are opening the business as a very part-time occupation—for instance, only creating product during the summer fresh-fruit growing season—you will need to forecast your financial future. Consider where you would like to be, financially, with your business in one year and in five years, and include that information here.

warning

Don't consider your business plan just a document necessary for obtaining financing that you rarely look at again. A business plan can be a strategic plan for your business that should be looked at and updated with some regularity.

Buying Equipment and Inventory

We'll cover specific food-related equipment in other parts of this book, but there are some basic office equipment needs for any small business, whatever the industry. There are some must-haves and there are some it-would-be-nice-to-haves for your business to operate efficiently and effectively.

warning

Remember to add a percentage of your fixed costs to the fee you charge for your products or catering services! This is how you pay the bills.

Essential Equipment

Whatever the location of your food-making operation (see Chapter 7 for a full discussion on location), you need to carve out some office-type space. It doesn't need to be a lot of space but it needs to be enough to enable you to be comfortable doing things like invoicing, ordering, and financial planning. If you don't like doing those things to begin with, you definitely won't want to do them in a place that is uncomfortable, cramped, or disorganized.

Basic office equipment includes:

▶ *Desk.* An office desk should be large enough for you to spread out and look at several things at once, whether it's numerous spreadsheets or a laptop and spreadsheet, or catalogs and your laptop and the spreadsheet that tells you how much you budgeted to spend on whatever you are ordering.

▶ *Phone.* Cell phones have often replaced the need for a landline phone. However, some people still prefer to have a landline for their business contact line where messages can be left. Then your cellphone can be used for times when you are away from your office. If you do decide to have a landline installed in your office, be sure it has a built-in voicemail function (almost standard these days). You probably also want a cordless option, depending on the size of your office space.

▶ *Other furniture.* At least one file cabinet will help you keep organized. You can add cabinets as you need them, but at some point you will only want to keep files in your office that are active or relatively new; you can put the rest in storage boxes in a closet or other storage area. Although you likely won't spend a lot of time at your desk in the food business, it is still a good idea to have a comfortable, ergonomic chair. If you may have a visitor in your office—a salesperson, potential client, or potential employee—make sure to have a couple of side chairs. A lot of great office furniture can be found at surplus sales.

▶ *Computer.* A decent computer that is either new or no more than a year old will allow you to save money doing some of your marketing and advertising materials yourself. A laptop or even a tablet may be sufficient. Once again, however, make sure you get a keyboard and any accessories that will help make it ergonomic and comfortable for you to use. See "The Best Computer" on page 72 for more specifics on computer purchasing.

▶ *Internet access.* Not only will you need internet service from your telecommunications provider and a modem to access the internet, a wireless router is highly recommended. They are inexpensive (in the range of $100), eliminate the need for a cord from your computer to the modem, and allow any type of computer to tap into the wireless service within its range. If your office is in a large retail space or your food prep area and the area is large, you may also want to consider a booster to allow you strong wireless access in the full area. Or simply budget for a tech-savvy consultant to do this all for you!

▶ *Printer*. If you plan to do some of your marketing and advertising materials yourself, a good printer is essential. The equipment itself is relatively inexpensive—these days you can buy a printer that produces high-quality printing as well as scans, copies, and faxes for under $150. However, the ink cartridges are where you will spend the money. Two rounds of black and color ink replacement cartridges, and you will have already spent the same as the cost of the printer itself. While you are at it, make sure to get a fast print speed of 15 to 20 black pages per minute.

▶ *Camera*. Phone cameras are such high quality these days that you may not find the need to have more than that. And that is especially true if you plan to hire a photographer to take shots of your finished work for marketing and advertising purposes. That said, a basic digital SLR with a couple of different lens sizes can be had for under $500 and seems to always be a worthwhile investment.

▶ *Software*. The basic Microsoft Office suite of Word, Excel, PowerPoint, and Access typically provides all you will ever need in the range of word processing, spreadsheet production, marketing and presentation software. The possibilities are endless for using these software tools these days, from a stripped-down version for your iPad like DocstoGo that costs around $15, to several hundred dollars for a full suite for your personal desktop or for multiple computers. Don't forget to sign up for some kind of antivirus software; free malware is available, or for under $100 per year you can get a subscription to Norton AntiVirus or other protection, which is essential in today's electronic world.

Use Figure 6–2 on page 71 as a shopping guide for equipping your office with supplies. You probably already have some of these and some you may not want to use—for

> **tip** ⓘ
>
> Brand recognition is the name of the game in business. It is typically worth the cost to have a graphic design firm design a logo for you. They will make your logo memorable, professional, and unique. Clip art can look tacky and may show up in another food-related business's materials. When you have your logo, be sure to use it in everything about your business, from business cards to website to food labels.

Office Supplies Checklist

❏ Postage scale

❏ Postage meter or stamps

❏ Paper for fax and copy machine

❏ Toner and ink cartridges for fax machine, copy machine, and computer printer

❏ "Sticky" notes in an assortment of sizes

❏ Scratch and telephone message pads

❏ Wastebaskets

❏ Scissors, Exacto® knives, staplers

❏ Three-ring binders and file folders

❏ Pens, pencils, tape, paper cutter, etc.

❏ Envelopes and stationery with your logo/company name

❏ Return envelopes with your address preprinted

❏ Wall safe for storing valuable papers, cash, and computer backup disks

❏ Time clock and cards

❏ Digital camera

❏ Measuring wheel and 100-foot tape measure

❏ Marking paint and long-handled paint gun

❏ Business cards

❏ Surge protectors for computers

❏ Calculators

❏ Calendars and/or planners

❏ CD and/or DVD disks and/or thumb drives

❏ Desk organizers

❏ Office furniture: desks, chairs, chair mats, file cabinets, conference table and chairs, computer workstations, lamps, shelving

❏ Fire extinguishers and first aid kit

❏ Coffee machine and microwave

❏ Janitorial and bathroom supplies

FIGURE 6–2: **Office Supplies Checklist**

example, fax machines are slowly fading out of use with scanners being part of even the simplest printers, but some businesses still use faxes so you may find it is a purchase you need to make.

After you've done your shopping (not buying, just shopping!), fill in the purchase price next to each item, add up your costs, and you'll have a head start on estimating your startup costs. Of course, this is not a complete list of supplies that you may need, so tailor it to what you think you will use.

▶ The Best Computer

These days you are almost able to get away with having nothing more than a tablet computer to run a business. A tablet can perhaps handle enough basic software, email, and internet searches to allow you to operate your business efficiently and effectively. They are portable and inexpensive—spend a little more and you don't even need wifi—satellite connection will allow you to use it almost anywhere, anytime.

A laptop is the next best thing. Laptops are powerful and can be quite small. They can use more complicated software. And they are no longer considerably more expensive than desktop computers to get similar storage and speed.

Desktop computers have come a long way as well. No longer the computer of choice, desktops have had to adapt to the portable world where users can get a lot out of their smartphones, which have become minitablets. Desktop computers, or at least their monitors, are going in the opposite direction—instead of more compact, monitors seem to be getting larger and larger. If you are going to have your computer tied to your desk, you might as well have something that is highly visible and can give you lots of space to create on. Computers like the HP Envy has a 23" touch screen that functions like a tablet and has the CPU housed within the monitor so it is sleek, without cords everywhere, but unlike most tablets, has USB ports for thumb drives and other accessories. It also has a movable arm attached to its screen which means you can move the monitor for the most comfortable position for you, including standing.

Computers like the Envy are great if your business requires you to do a lot of design work where you may be sitting at your desk a lot or if you plan to do a lot of your back-office tasks such as bookkeeping and supply ordering yourself.

Do your research online, then utilize the personnel of places like Best Buy, Staples, or local computer businesses to help you decide which choice is best for you. Your computer is not likely to be your largest expenditure, but it could be the item you purchase that you use the most every day.

▶ Purchasing an Existing Business

Perhaps you are thinking about starting your own specialty food business by purchasing one that already exists. Maybe you have patronized this business many times, have always been attracted to it, and feel like you could do it better, take it to the next level. This is the way many business owners get into business. But you likely need to be prepared to jump right in pretty quickly.

Here are a few things to think about when purchasing an existing business:

▶ You will definitely want to set aside funding for legal help for the due diligence that is important in researching an existing business.

▶ Make a marketing plan for the turnover of the business so that you can be sure to retain existing customers. Will customers jump ship because the existing owner is so popular and equated with the business? Or will prior customers come back because they have been dissatisfied but are willing to try out the business under new management?

▶ If the current owner is popular and an asset to the business, be sure to build in a transition period where the owner continues with the business for a certain amount of time.

Another way to purchase an existing business, or more precisely purchase *into* an existing business, is to buy a franchise. Look on "franchiseopportunities.com" under "Gourmet and Specialty Franchises" and other franchise sales websites to see if something fits what you are interested in. Pizza, frozen yogurt, and barbecue are a few commonly franchised specialty foods as well as a few better-known shops like Edible Arrangements and Cold Stone Creamery.

Step into the franchise world with your eyes wide open. While it can be a great way to enter the specialty foods market, it also can be expensive and restrictive. Plan to have a lawyer look over a franchise contract and tell you exactly what you are committing to.

Inventory

Inventory for a food business will also vary widely depending on the business you plan to start. Again, we will discuss food-specific inventory later in this book. But at this stage you will want to think through your nonperishables and hard goods required to start up and get your business established.

You will need bowls and dishes and measuring tools and storage containers, etc. But will you need displayware for your finished product—either those that are ready for sampling in your showroom or the food items you take to an event? If you are selling food items in a gift basket, you will need lots of inventory to create the final baskets—from the basket itself to the stuffer material, to rolls of cellophane for covering, to ribbon and even scissors to cut the ribbon.

warning

Don't buy huge amounts of inventory of things like gift wrap or baskets unless, for example, you can get a ridiculously good deal on large quantities of a classic basket. Colors and designs go in and out of style. You don't want to be stuck with years of inventory on something that you used only a portion of, only to have it get dusty and old-looking, not to mention taking up precious space.

Home Is Where the Stove Is: Location

W hether your specialty food business operates out of your home only selling to your personal friends, has a retail shop as a minor component of the business, provides retail outlets with product, or is a direct-to-consumer national mail order operation will, of course, have a major impact on what type of location you need to set up shop in. This chapter will take each one into consideration.

Cottage Food Industry

Let's start with the smallest of possible specialty food setups—food produced in the home, known as the "cottage food industry." While this may be small in regard to the size of each individual business, it is by no means small in overall size within the food industry. The Harvard Food Law and Policy Clinic states that "the past few years have seen a marked increase in the amount of local and small-scale food production in the United States" ("Cottage Food Laws in the United States," August 2013). Accompanying this increase "has come a push to allow individuals to produce and sell nonpotentially hazardous foods [baked goods, jams, jellies, e.g.] made in their home kitchens, outside of expensive permitting and licensing procedures. . . . therefore reducing the barriers to entry for small-scale producers while recognizing the low-risk nature of these products."

By definition, a cottage business is set up in the home. And while there is no restriction that you have a commercial kitchen in which you make your product, it does not mean there are not rules to follow. And it typically means that it is difficult to sell your product across state lines since even states that permit cottage food businesses have differing regulations.

How you proceed from the cottage business definition is up to you and the laws in your state. You do not need a commercial kitchen (although the next section outlines what is entailed and how one of our specialty food mentors did create a commercial kitchen in her home) and typically you do not even have to have your home kitchen inspected. However, that does not mean that you don't want to consider the things that will be important to you and the success of your business such as:

> ► Is your kitchen set up in some efficient way conducive to creating food products for sale?
> ► Are other family members okay with your plans for a food business operated out of your home?
> ► Is your family's schedule conducive to your using the family kitchen for a food business? Are your

aha!

Even though you operate your specialty food business from your home, you should still set your business up as a legal entity, carry insurance on the business, and keep your financials for your business separate from your personal financials.

—"10 Tips for Starting a Home-Based Food Business" by Jennifer Goforth Gregory, for *The News & Observer* spouse and children off to work and school all day making the 9 A.M. to 2 P.M. time period a great time to do the cooking for your business?

▶ Is there a place in your home environment to store the supplies you will need to create your food product? Don't forget it's not just food items you will need, but you may need food containers, boxes, oversized cooking vessels, extra utensils, etc.

▶ Does your home have a place that can be set up exclusively for the office work of the business, even if that is just a desk in the corner of the dining room that no one will disturb?

▶ Does UPS, FedEx, and other carriers know how to get to your house? Can you get things shipped to you in a timely manner? Does your area have overnight priority or even Saturday delivery available? This might be more important than you realize!

tip

If you want good advice on equipment, go to the website of America's Test Kitchen. There you will find equipment reviews. And you can find out where in your region ATK's TV show is on or watch it on the website. These folks put cooking utensils, appliances, and all kinds of cookware to the test— everything from bench scrapers to cookie presses to colanders.

—www.americas testkitchen.com

Supplies for Your Homebased Food Business

First and foremost, if you are going to be serious about your food enterprise, you should use separate supplies, utensils, and cookware for your business than for your family cooking. You perhaps won't want two microwave ovens or two baking ovens, but a cupboard set aside for other items is a good idea.

Buy as high quality as you can afford. You can always trade up when you start to bring in some income—that's what is meant by using the income in your first couple years to reinvest in the business.

Don't just think about the equipment you need but also think about what can make you more efficient. Sure, you can get by with a hand mixer for quite a while but what else could you be doing if you weren't standing there holding the mixer, but instead had a KitchenAid countertop mixer?

What you will need depends a lot on what you are planning to make for your specialty food. Some basics include:

▶ Mixing bowls

- ▶ Measuring cups
- ▶ Measuring spoons
- ▶ Spatulas
- ▶ Large spoons
- ▶ A set of knives
- ▶ A knife sharpener
- ▶ Egg separator
- ▶ Spreading knives
- ▶ Pastry cutter
- ▶ Frosting bag and tips
- ▶ Prep bowls (those little Pyrex bowls that you can measure things out ahead of time and just dump in when the time is right)
- ▶ Corian cutting boards of different sizes
- ▶ Baking pans (different sizes as well as glass and metal)
- ▶ Cookie sheets of varying sizes
- ▶ Muffin tins, mini and traditional sized cups
- ▶ Cooling racks
- ▶ Frying pans (several sizes)
- ▶ Microwave oven
- ▶ Mixer with variety of attachments
- ▶ Food processor
- ▶ Grinder
- ▶ Graters

warning

If you are planning to start a cottage food business, read the brochure "Cottage Food Laws in the United States" by Harvard Food Law and Policy Clinic in its entirety at http://blogs. law.harvard.edu. While all states are different and you need to research the laws in your individual state, this brochure will give you a broad overview of potential laws and their purpose.

The list could go on much longer, but much of what you will need will depend on what kind of food you plan to make. Jams and jellies will require different preparation tools than baked goods like whoopie pies or specialty cakes. Some foods will require frying pans and stovetop ware, others will require baking pans and egg beaters.

The Commercial Kitchen

The dreaded "commercial kitchen" does not have to be dreaded at all. If you want to do anything more than a simple food business selling to your personal friends, you will need to embrace the idea that the kitchen you operate out of needs to be of a grade that would at the very least pass inspection by a licensing body in your state. In Washington State, for example, where our mentor Susan Desjardins Burns and her Confectionately Yours toffee business is located, "no food service can be approved in a home kitchen, unless there are two separate kitchens. A commercial kitchen must be totally separate from the kitchen used by the people who live there."

Susan tried first renting commercial kitchen space but got frustrated with the lack of attention to cleanliness and detail from other renters of the space. She decided if she was going to make the toffee operation a success, she was going to need her own commercial kitchen. Susan went about carefully researching everything she needed to know and keeping in touch with the food safety authorities who would be inspecting and giving the kitchen the stamp of approval. She took no chances that her kitchen would not be approved—if she had a question, she didn't guess the answer, she asked. And now her garage has been transformed into a commercial kitchen a step away from home.

warning

Many states that allow for cottage food businesses still require that certain regulations are followed such as that it is the actual seller who is producing the food and that labels indicate that the food was not processed in a commercial kitchen subject to health department inspections. Some states have limits on gross annual sales.

▶ Homestead Food Operations

Prior to June 2012, home food manufacturing in New Hampshire required a homestead license. In June 2012, the state signed legislation changing the licensing requirements for home food operations. Now, you do not need a homestead food license if:

▶ You sell nonpotentially hazardous (which mostly means cooked products but even some of those are not legal to make at home) only from your own residence

▶ You do not exceed gross annual sales of $20,000

Still required, however, is proper labeling that includes the name, address, and phone of your operation, ingredients in descending order of predominance by weight, any major food allergen, a product code which identifies batch number, and the phrase "This product is exempt from New Hampshire licensing and inspection" in at least 10-point font. (source: NH Department of Health and Human Services, www.dhhs.state.nh.us)

You can see that even with more lenient regulations such as the homestead license in New Hampshire, it is still important to check with your licensing health department and make sure you are doing everything absolutely legally for your food business.

The main focus of a commercial kitchen is the creation of safe food products—and who wouldn't want to guarantee their customers as safe a product as possible? Think stainless steel—countertops, appliances—that don't harbor food contaminants and is highly cleanable. Other considerations are getting running water and dishwasher water to a high enough temperature to kill any bacteria.

A commercial kitchen is not cheap but it also doesn't have to be cost-prohibitive. Burns' garage renovation commercial kitchen came in at around $24,000. Obviously it is not the right move for a very small operation that never plans to get bigger—it's going to take a lot of cupcakes to break even on a $24,000 investment. However, in an example like Confectionately Yours, you can also count in the potential added value to your home.

These are some key things to think about before deciding to use your home as your base of operations. A good thing to do is visualize a busy day in the life of your business from start to finish and think through everything that might come up in that day. Also, talk with a couple of people who have been there, done that. Ask for the good and the bad stories. Then decide if your home has, or can have, all the right stuff from which to operate.

Of course, the idea of a zero commute can be very appealing and can add to the profit you can make on your business. On the other hand, a zero commute means you can find yourself in your home 24 hours a day. You might want to make sure to schedule mixing it up a little. Depending on how much product you plan to sell, you could set aside two days a week to make product, two days a week to bring it to wherever you plan to sell it, and one half day a week doing your bookkeeping and supplies ordering.

One thing about working from your home on your own small business is the beauty of flexibility. While you need to be serious about your business to make it successful, don't trap yourself into not enjoying the flexibility this setup should afford you.

The Retail Shop

A specialty food business that is focused on selling at retail will mean that from the outset you will be looking for the best location and type of physical space for a retail operation. Retail is a very special business type where you have a set base of operations and the expectation is that your customers will find you, visit your shop, and buy your products.

Are you a high-end specialty food business? Locate in an area with specialty boutiques—Main Street downtown or an upscale shopping mall. More day-to-day food like bread or cupcakes? You can still produce a topnotch, upscale product but an individual cupcake or loaf of bread is still accessibly priced so a busy location along a main thoroughfare might work fine.

Outside

Your storefront will be the first impression your customer gets of your business—unless they found you on the internet, in which case your website will be their first impression. Of course, if you enticed them with a fabulous website that is professional and classy, your store had better live up to their expectations. A customer could drive to your location excited by what they saw on your website only to be turned away from ever entering your door because the view from the street is rundown, dirty, sloppy, or just simply not what they were expecting. Branding your business includes keeping with a particular style from your computer presence to your physical presence as well as the look of your product labeling. For example, if you decide on a country primitive style

fun fact ☺

No matter where you set up shop, if you are hanging your toque on sustainability, recyclability, and fair trade you need to be aware of the trends and places in your business where this matters. Even the big companies pay attention to these trends—Nestlé announced that beginning in 2016, "cocoa used in the formulation of its KitKat branded bars will be sustainably sourced" according to "Nestlé Shifting KitKat Brand to Sustainably Sourced Cocoa" in *Food Business News'* online magazine, September 8, 2015.

for your product labels, it would be inconsistent to have your physical store showcase a contemporary, artsy look.

Landscape in front of your store—even if that just means a couple of whiskey barrels with flowers in them—but if you do, make sure the landscaping is kept neat and the plants are watered. Dead plants in broken wood barrels with trash littering them are a sign of how the rest of your business is run.

A leased site means you need to make sure the landlord keeps up with fixing broken stairs, cracked concrete, and difficult doorknobs. If you choose to buy or even if you lease, make sure the windows are always clean (a window cleaning service is typically worth the money). If you are open, make sure the "open/closed" sign is turned the right way. These all may seem like small things, but turning customers off before they ever get a chance to sample your exquisite whoopie pies is not a way to make a business thrive.

Inside

Once you get them in the door, you need to once again wow them with your appearance. Food businesses have an extra special need to appear squeaky clean. Make sure displays are fresh—so don't create display areas so huge that it is expensive, time consuming, and takes a lot of product to keep them appetizing.

Be sure to leave room to browse around and for customers to not feel crowded, which just encourages them to leave quickly. If you are a one-, or at most, two-person shop, many times (hopefully) you will be tied up with customers either in front of you or on the phone (more on that in a minute). Make sure there is enough on display to browse to keep a customer occupied for a few minutes while you finish up with your customer.

You'll want to decide on a look before you start outfitting the public area of your retail shop. If you want a vintage feel, use some antique tables and thrift shop doilies for display. If contemporary is your style, you can use modern furnishings with bold colors as backdrops. Maybe you would like a theme—or even to change themes with the seasons. Best to use basic furnishings that won't give off one style or another but will let you use decorations to create the look.

warning ⚠

If your retail food business includes take-home meals and you cook aromatic foods for prepared meals, you do not want to locate your business next to a fancy dress shop. You will soon have a disgruntled neighbor who is unhappy that their haute couture smells like your haute cuisine. If the fancy dress shop moves in next to you, well, they probably should have done a little more homework!

Whatever you decide, keep the shop clean, dust and dirt free, smelling fresh, and looking tidy. No one wants to buy food in a store that seems dirty or smells bad.

Special Display Needs

Some retail items do need specialty displays to show them off at their best. Greeting cards, for instance, are best displayed in racks that are designed for greeting cards. These racks are specially made to take up the smallest amount of space to display the cards. You may think you can display cards in baskets, and you certainly can. But as they are taken in and out of the basket to look at them, you risk their getting bent edges, which makes the next customer not as likely to purchase the card. Special display racks can end up being worth the extra cost not only because they show off the item at its best but because they often display more of the item in a smaller space, leaving room for other product.

And speaking of customers, it is critical to be able to juggle more than one customer at a time. So if you are in the midst of working with a customer on an order of whoopie pies for their wedding and another potential customer walks in the door, at least acknowledge the new customer. Once a person in your shop has been personally engaged, it is more uncomfortable for them to walk out. And if you are going to be a while with your wedding whoopie pie customer, excuse yourself for a moment and go talk with the new customer—perhaps they just wanted to grab a couple whoopie pies to bring home for a treat or they wanted to pick up a brochure or they wanted to know if you ship across the country. You may be able to quickly answer their question and get back to your wedding customer and keep both customers satisfied.

Phone conversations are similar. Priority should go to the person who has taken the time to walk in your door. If business over the phone is a significant part of

warning

You can't get away from politics, Congress, and legislation, even in the specialty food business. *Food Business News* reports in their September 8, 2015, issue that food safety programs are threatening to be funded by user fees, considerably increasing food businesses' fees, rather than through appropriated funds.

save

You don't have to purchase new equipment—often you can get a higher level of equipment or display space by purchasing used. Shops go out of business all the time. You can capitalize on their need to sell their equipment, or check out state surplus outlets and, of course, online listings for deals. Just make sure to buy what you need and not just what happens to be out there at a good price. It's not a good deal if it doesn't suit your purpose.

your business, you need to invest in the personnel so that someone can deal exclusively with in-person customers while someone else focuses on phone orders. Once again, if you are the one-person shop, acknowledge your walk-in customer, excuse yourself from the phone for a minute to see if there is something you can do for the walk-in customer to get them on their way, or get the phone customer's number and call them back after retail hours so you can give them your undivided attention and give the walk-in customers the attention they deserve.

Back Office

The back office area of a gourmet food retail shop may include a place where food is actually produced for sale on the retail floor. This means giving careful consideration to any space you look at for a potential retail space. If the space seems absolutely perfect for the retail operation you envision, perhaps you can think through whether there is a way to have the production space somewhere else. If you are doing large-scale production, that may be a necessity. A large warehouse-style setup for production may have a great retail space opportunity but is rarely in an area that is conducive to a retail market. Vice versa, a good retail space rarely has an area large enough for large-scale production. But then you might get lucky; you never know unless you look and ask around.

Back office functions also include the space to do the unavoidable paperwork of any business. You might be able to get away with a hybrid operation where you have your retail space, and your deskwork is done from a corner of the living room at home.

aha!

If you are opening a specialty food business in the bakery category, you may be surprised to find yourself suddenly interested in wheat futures and bakery ingredient indexes. *Food Business News* will keep you up to date, either in their print magazine or online edition at www. foodbusinessnews.net.

The Retail Provider

Perhaps you are totally into creating your unique whoopie pies but you do not want to be burdened with a retail space to sell them from. You arrange with a retail shop in each of the surrounding five towns to provide them with fresh product daily. And you are selling direct to consumers for special events, weddings, anniversary parties, and other private functions.

This is a great scenario where you get to focus on the part you love—food production. In this case, you would need to find a location where production of the food is the focus of the space. It might mean a commercial kitchen is already set up, or that you need

stat fact

The U.S. Food and Drug Administration Food Code is a model code and reference document intended for use by state and local governments regarding food safety laws. This is not law and states are not required to adopt the code but many do.

to be able to renovate an existing kitchen to make it a commercially licensed kitchen, or create one from scratch (see section on commercial kitchens earlier in this chapter). Unless you are buying the space—which can be a great way to build business assets—be sure to negotiate leasehold improvements (see "The Lease" on page 87 for more tips) to create the space you require to be successful (and to be able to pay the rent!).

Staging Space

In an operation like this, where production of the product is the focus, you will still need to have storage space for supplies for both making the whoopie pies and for packaging them for shipment to your retail outlets. And your space will need to include a clean, open space for the actual packaging and arranging into shipment lots.

Getting Product to Market

Perhaps you have five outlets—one in your own town and one in each of four surrounding towns—that will regularly carry your whoopie pies. The contract with each is that you will make deliveries to them twice a week on specific days. Your personal vehicle may be perfect for this—a minivan or one of those square cargo-like vehicles like a Kia Soul or Honda Element. Just don't use your personal vehicle that your two golden retrievers thrash around in on your daily trips to walk them on the beach. This would make a vehicle a very legitimate part of your startup financing.

Mail Order

While some foods—delicate pastries, for example—are not conducive to the mail order market, many specialty food businesses start out with a retail outlet and add mail order to their business offerings. Winnipesaukee Chocolates in Wolfeboro, New Hampshire, does

tip

BakingBusiness.com online magazine shared tips on how to identify the trends that are here to stay for a while. In an interview for the article "Expo East 2015: Identifying the Next Big Thing," Eric Pierce, director of strategy for New Hope Natural Media, points to something he calls "consumption occasions." How many consumers and opportunities for consumption comprise the product demand?

shipping but states on its website that they do not ship their chocolates during warm weather months where the temperatures are consistently in excess of 75 degrees (specifically June to mid-September) because they have not set their business up with the extra packaging needs that warm weather shipping would require. Although a puddle of chocolate would probably taste just fine, it would not represent the beautiful presentation that Winnipesaukee Chocolates has worked so hard to create.

You may want to open a specialty food business that is exclusively mail order. That is a completely legitimate and potentially lucrative approach to your business. But what does that mean as far as location? It probably means you can set up your business just about anywhere. But there are some considerations.

Shipping Service

If you plan to be completely mail order, you will want to be located in a place that is accessible for the kind of courier/shipping service you need to be able to come to your business site. It wouldn't take too many times standing in line at the USPS or other courier shipping locations for you to realize that your time could be better spent if the shipper came to you.

Depending on your size, you may need to pick a location that has a loading dock. If you are shipping out pallet-sized shipments each day, the shipper will want to back up to your loading dock.

Special Considerations

If you have a product that requires refrigeration, this will have implications on both the shipper that you can use and the area that you hold your packages until the shipper arrives. That area may need to be at the very least cooled or perhaps even refrigerated. You may even want to locate a walk-in cooler near the loading dock where product is stored while awaiting the shipper.

tip

Like any industry, the food industry has its own terms. For instance, "potentially hazardous food" typically is determined by the acidity of the food and whether the food is likely to develop bacteria or viruses. High-acid foods like tomatoes and certain cooked items have a low potential for being hazardous while meats, seafood, and dairy have high potential to be hazardous.

tip

When choosing a carrier for fragile product, be sure to choose one that has experience shipping fragile items. You might check around with other purveyors of your type of product to see who they use and what their experiences have been.

Fragile items may also require special needs. This might be in the form of packaging. At the very least, you will need a package that indicates it is fragile and what kind of special handling it needs—do not tip, always carry with this side up, etc. It may even require you to go so far as ordering special packaging inserts such as circular cardboard loops that hold cupcakes or mini cheesecakes upright.

tip

Put "customer" in the forefront of your mind when thinking about a retail space. If yours is a high-end product, where do those customers typically shop? What kind of parking do you need to make your location convenient to that customer base you wish to draw?

► The Lease

Unless you are setting up in your existing home, chances are you will lease a retail or production space rather than purchase a building—at least at the beginning. There are a few important things to remember when negotiating a lease contract:

- ► Be realistic about the time frame of the lease. The SBA recommends that small businesses negotiate one- or two-year leases with the option to renew.

- ► Whatever that first lease agreement says will be the starting point for yearly lease negotiations from here on out for the rest of the life of the lease. Don't start at the top amount you can possibly afford since you can be certain that your lease will only go up, not down.

- ► Make sure it is clearly spelled out who is responsible for everything, such as leasehold improvements, which light fixtures (e.g., exterior lights may be for more than just your space so the leaseholder should probably cover those), the plumbing, etc. The SBA says be sure to look for hidden fees and that CAMs (Common Area Maintenance) are covered by landlords.

- ► One of the benefits of leasing over owning is that when something goes wrong, you can call the leaseholder. Not only should you make sure that person is accessible or has a property manager who is accessible, but the SBA recommends that you make sure that the landlord and not the tenant is actually responsible for the maintenance since it is not the same as with residential leases.

- ► Always spend the money to have a lawyer look over something as important as a long-term lease.

Distributors

Perhaps you are planning to create your specialty food and ship it out to other distributors that take it to the retail market that they service. You can create a setup similar to a mail order center with the difference being that your shipments will be a lot larger than your individual mail order packages. You will need a larger space that accommodates a warehouse-type setup. While you should heed the advice of this book's mentors and start small, look at the space you choose with an eye to the future. Is there any chance your business could grow while staying right where it is? Or do you go into your initial space fully aware that it is likely you will need to move in order to expand?

Food Labels

The Food and Drug Administration controls food labeling under the Federal Food, Drug, and Cosmetic Act and its amendments. According to the FDA's website, food labeling is required for most prepared foods, such as breads, cereals, canned and frozen foods, snacks, desserts, drinks, etc. It is your job to keep up with labeling requirements and find out what is necessary for your product. The FDA states that uniform compliance to food labeling regulations that were issued in 2015 and 2016 is by January 1, 2018. Bookmark their website at www.fda.gov/Food/default.htm and check the site at least quarterly to find out if any new regulations will impact the specialty food category your business falls under.

tip

If at all possible, lease a space that is a bit larger than what you think you currently need. Few business owners start out with no plans for growth. The first few years of your business venture you will likely be growing exponentially while customers find you and the word gets out—you don't want to be spending your startup years moving from place to place to accommodate every growth spurt.

All Things Digital

Although Facebook and other social media platforms are constantly offering new and creative ways to reach out to constituents, there is no substitute yet for the good "old-fashioned" website. A well-thought-out website with a design that reflects your business style is a must.

Here are some basic things to keep in mind about a website for your business:

▶ Websites give you the ability to change content quickly and cheaply, making it easy to keep information up-to-date and showcase the latest items you have to offer. Printing a brochure does not afford you that ease of change—to keep costs down, brochures need to be printed in high numbers, meaning you may still have hundreds left when you want to change something on it. You will need to decide whether to pay to have your website designer change content or learn how to do it yourself.

▶ Customers can readily get information, or more information, about your business just by looking at your website. In the food industry, this might mean weeding out a lot of phone calls from those who quickly discover you are not for them, saving you time to focus on production or the customers actually in your store instead of talking on the phone.

▶ You can track the results of your marketing efforts more easily with website "hits," questions, and follow-through sales you get from your site.

▶ You are open 24/7/365.

Mobile Websites

Mobile-device-friendly websites have been around awhile. With the use of smartphones for web searching continuing to increase and the closer we get to the wrist-worn smartphone being in common use, the world is on the verge of a yet another paradigm shift in the way we use computers. Creating a website that is more easily viewed on these smaller devices can be a smart move.

Many people still choose to download the entire website no matter what device they are using, so if you don't want to spend the money on having a separate site created, it's not the end of the world. However, the more easily used your website is, the more it will be used.

Setting Up a Website

If you are adept at computer software and want to design your own website, you might be perfectly suited to creating your own site, especially if it's going to be an information-only site that won't need the complications of interactive features.

However, no matter who designs your website, you need to be sure it is professional looking. Just like when you are meeting a potential customer in person, you need your website to express your business's style and culture. Check out websites of food business in your same category and take notes on what they offer that you think is a must and what is not so pertinent to your business or customers.

If you don't feel like you can create the right website, don't hesitate to hire a professional web design company. The cost is not necessarily out of reach, but be sure to hire a company with the ability to do what you want it to do. You will also incur monthly charges to have it "hosted"—someone with a large server keeps everything coming and going. Hosting fees can range from as little as $30 a month to several hundred, depending on the complexity of your web business.

Usually included in the hosting fee is a certain amount of monthly changes. However, it is highly recommended that you not only learn to make changes to your website yourself but also that your contract allows for you to do that. This is critical, even if it requires sending a staff person to a class to learn HTML or whatever language your website operates with. Internet users today expect websites to be dynamic. Most food businesses change up their products regularly. If you have a storefront, your hours may change seasonally, you may constantly be running new events, or you may want to showcase publicity you are receiving, so keeping your website up-to-date with all this changing information is a must.

Design

Before you hire a designer, look at lots of other websites and give the designer ideas on what you like and don't like. Your designer will likely provide you with a few options that you can choose from, either in their entirety or plucking bits and pieces from each.

Find web designers by searching online or noticing who designed the sites you like. The designer doesn't have to be local to design your site—everything can be done, well, online!

You can also buy "template" web designs—you fill the details into a basic design. There are many template companies to choose from, such as weebly. com, web.com, wordpress.org, or baskweb.com, which includes a shopping cart system. You don't have to be a computer programming wiz as they are designed to be put together by anyone with basic computer skills. Some wireless networks offer the ability to create a website through them. GoDaddy and other domain hosting sites also have templates, although they may cost a modest fee to use.

tip

Using a template doesn't mean you need to or should create a cookie cutter website—creative and changing content will make your site stand on its own.

But if your business is a little complex, pay the price for having one designed by a professional. Perhaps your business is not complex now, but who knows what the future holds. If you have plans to expand, you will want a website that can easily expand with you.

The design of your site should be simple yet comprehensive. By the time people have spent a few minutes on your website, they should have a pretty good sense of what you offer—and whether your business is the right one for their needs.

If your business has a mail order component, you will need to have your designer figure out the best shopping cart platform and cash-out system for your type of consumer. Shoppers expect to be able to do the whole shopping experience, soup to nuts, online.

Website Must-Haves

As you create your website, these are "must-haves":

- ▶ Homepage
- ▶ "Contact Us" page
- ▶ "About Us" page
- ▶ Testimonials from customers. Use real names (only with permission), not initials after the quotes, if possible.
- ▶ Photos (make sure you have permission from not only the photographer but from any recognizable people)
- ▶ Your business's logo and address. If your business is a retail location, your address should appear on all of the pages of your website—don't make people dig for the basic information they want/need or to figure out whose website they are on and where you are.

warning

There is no quicker way to undermine your credibility than to maintain a sloppy website. Be sure that words are not misspelled. Misspelled words reflect carelessness and a lack of professionalism. It's worth spending a few bucks to pay someone to proofread your site before going live. And keep it up-to-date. Outdated information makes you look like you are out of business.

The Homepage

Viewers will first come to your "homepage" (also called a "landing page" if this is where a search will land viewers) where you will introduce them to your business and tempt them to spend some time on your site browsing other pages—and ultimately be enticed enough to pick up the phone and place an order, visit your retail location, or whatever it is you hope to inspire them to do by visiting your website.

You should include a short "Our Story" section either right on your home page or in a drop down menu. This is chance for people to feel like they understand your business, can relate to you, and therefore want to do business with you—but don't go into such detail that you lose them right at the homepage!

Be catchy but avoid being too clever. The web customer should open to your site and immediately know they got what they are looking for. Be sure your name and contact information is right there (you would be surprised by websites that don't have the business name on every page, including the home page, leaving viewers wondering whose site they are on!). Be sure any pictures are of the highest quality to reflect the quality of your goods.

tip

Update the look of your website every couple of years, perhaps, but don't change it so often that repeat viewers aren't sure if they got to your site or not. And when you do plan to update, plan to provide some teasers a couple months in advance so your regular customers and viewers know to expect a different look.

You don't need and don't want to show everything you do right at the start. First off, the "landing page" that the viewer comes to might take too long to download, which will be frustrating and cause the viewer to move on to the next thing before you are able to snag him into looking more into your business. Keep the homepage simple but informative.

Include a menu of items along one edge of your homepage—top or either side—with headings that the viewer can click on to get to that section of your site. Think of it like the signs you see overhead in the grocery store or the pharmacy—direct people to the sections they are interested in. The person who came to your site probably has one specific interest—catering menus, your retail schedule, what your next batch of fresh jam is going to be—and doesn't want to have to view everything you are up to. Make it easy for the website visitor to find what is particularly relevant to them. Here are some ways to do that.

Drilling Down

Each time the viewer clicks a button on your website they get further into your site. This can be accomplished in two ways—one is with a "pop-up window" where, when they click on a category, the new section pops up over the main page and when they are finished browsing and close it out, they end up at the page they started from. The other "drills" them further and further into your site. Drilling down like this is a common way that websites are set up but it can get frustrating if the user can't easily get back to a point where they saw something they wanted to look at further. One way to help this is to always have a "home" link/button on every page—all they have to do is click "home" to get them back to the beginning and find their way forward again from there. It's like having Dorothy's ruby red slippers on your site at all times—unlike for poor Dorothy, make sure it's clear how easy it is to get home without having to deal with flying monkeys and sleep-inducing poppies before getting there.

The Rest of the Site

Your homepage is one of the most important parts of your website. If you don't capture your visitors at the homepage, they are unlikely to go any further than that. But if your homepage does what it needs to do, viewers landing there will be intrigued enough by your photos and your text to move to the other areas of your site.

warning

When writing the text for your website, be careful not to use "business speak." Terms like "POS" and "Deliverables" are not meaningful to the general public who is looking at your website.

If yours is a relatively complicated specialty food business, you want a button for each area of your business. For example, Stonewall Kitchens' website has buttons along the top that include "Specialty Foods," "Tableware," "Recipes," and "Barn Sale," among others. They also have a list of buttons down the side that expand upon those buttons and include things like "Cooking School" and "Corporate Gifts." This allows the viewer to really home in on that part of the business that she went to the site for to begin with. Now hopefully she will be intrigued enough to click on other things (like the yummy picture of "tropical fruit jam"), but if not, you haven't irritated the viewer having to dig for the pertinent information.

tip

Always include your business's name, address, and phone number on every page of your website. Once customers have drilled a few pages down into your site, they don't want to have to backtrack all the way back to your homepage just to get your contact information.

Most websites will have their overarching category buttons running across the top, since they will all appear when you open the site and won't run off the bottom of the page. If you only have a few categories, then that might not be an issue. Whatever you do, be sure it is designed as much for ease of use as for looks.

Contacting You from a Website

There was a time when websites were mainly marketing and information pieces—people came to the site to view what you do and offer, then called to talk with you directly. That is still an important role for a website. However, with the ease of use of today's technology, keep in mind that people are often browsing websites at 11:00 at night from the mobile phone while on the commuter train—they can't call you and speak to you then! If they have an impulse to contact you about placing an order, it should be possible to do that directly from your website.

For simple contact, be sure to have an email button. If you have employees but decide to have only one email address, be sure to have a mechanism in place to communicate to other employees email that is directed toward their function within the business.

warning

Few things will make a visitor click away from a website than finding outdated information. Keep anything that is time sensitive current and regularly change anything that makes your site appear dated, such as a reference to an event long past.

Updating

A good tool to make it clear to viewers that this is an active website is to have something on the site that requires a date—an archive of press releases, a copyright date that changes at least annually, or a link to your blog with current entries are some ways that visitors landing on your site see that it is current.

Nothing deters a viewer faster than going to a list of events that have all already happened—if you have a long list of events, it's fine to keep the old ones on to show viewers what they missed. Be sure there are always upcoming events listed, even if it's labeled "date to be determined." Have at least something that will show viewers that the site is being updated. If not, they will suspect that everything on the site might be old.

Marketing Your Website

Once you have created your website, don't keep it a secret! While your website may be in cyberspace, be sure your web address is on every printed piece you create for your business—letterhead, business cards, print advertisements, newsletters (print and enewsletters), radio ads—everything that has to do with your business should announce your web address. Put the address in your answering machine message. Make sure it is on the door of your storefront if you have one so anyone walking by who either doesn't have time to come in or wanders by during your off hours knows they can find you on the internet.

All of this is especially important if your web address is considerably different from your business name—which is not recommended, but sometimes can't be avoided, as in the instance that another or business has already taken a web domain name similar, or even the same, as your name.

Your Website URL

Your website has to have a unique address, called a URL or "domain name," that will be used on the server it resides on. Using the name of your business is your best choice; if another business is already using the name you've chosen for your business, pick the next closest name; sometimes just adding the town your business is in is sufficient—greatcupcakesboston.com

► Get People Clicking

There's no point to having a website if you don't do what you can to get people to click on it. Here are some tips for attracting customers to your website:

- ► Simply tell all your friends and family and ask them to tell all their friends and family.
- ► Do the appropriate search engine registration (some web services will do this for you).
- ► Make sure every printed and online piece you send to anyone has your website URL listed prominently.
- ► Suggest visitors bookmark your site.
- ► Trade web advertising with other websites.
- ► Create contests with giveaways that drive people to your site.
- ► Change your website content regularly to keep people coming back to see what's new.
- ► Join online discussion groups.
- ► If you do public speaking, always mention your site.
- ► Provide an "expert" column to newspapers and make sure to mention your website.
- ► Connect your website to social media links (see Chapter 12 on social media for other ideas).

These are just a few of a long list of ideas for getting people to come to your website in the first place, keep coming back, and to encourage them to tell everyone they know. Click around to websites in businesses similar to yours or in any category that interests you, see what catches your eye, and get other creative ideas to drive people to your site.

will immediately tell searchers that they have found you if someone already has greatcupcakes.com.

Domain names must be registered for a minimum of two years, after which you can renew them. The cost to register a name for two years is quite reasonable, typically under $100 per name. You will likely register with the suffix .com but you can also register .net and others (and even more suffixes are being created) even if you don't plan to use them so a similar businesses doesn't snatch it up. There are several companies that handle registration; GoDaddy and Domain.com are two well-known ones.

Keep 'Em Interested

Once you get visitors checking out your site, there are some ways to keep them there as long as possible. The longer they are there, the more likely they are to look at everything you have to offer and find something they would like to purchase—or tell their friends who are ready for a food purchase.

tip

It can't be emphasized enough how useful it is to spend time looking at other businesses' websites, particularly in your category, before you design your own—whether you do it yourself or hire a designer. Keep a checklist of what you like and don't like about these websites and incorporate these findings in your design plans. Choose colors, typefaces, and other stylistic elements that you feel work on other websites.

► Ethical (and Legal) Concerns

A brief word on copyright, fair use, and intellectual property concerns when it comes to your website.

It is not okay to use other people's writing, articles, blurbs, photos, and/or music on your website without permission. Just because it is on their website and in cyberspace and you are not printing or selling their work does not make it okay for you to use it for free. If there is something you really want to use, that you think is perfect for your website and what you are trying to get across, by all means attempt to gain permission to use it. But if you can't figure out who owns it or can't make contact with the owner/creator, find something else, create something yourself, or hire someone to create something that you will own and can use however you would like.

Be sure they know immediately whose website they have landed on. Make it easy for them to contact you by having a "contact us" button that makes it simple for them to send you a message.

Keep your website fun and changing. Do contests, puzzles, or whatever you can for fun interaction, but always connect it to your business.

Choosing a Web Host

You must select a service to host your website. Examples of well-known web hosts include DreamHost, GoDaddy, and HostGator, but there are many, many smaller hosts available.

Before choosing a web host, ask these questions:

- ▶ How often does the site go down?
- ▶ How long does it take to fix the site when it goes down?
- ▶ What is its customer support system?
- ▶ How many incoming lines does the server have?
- ▶ What is the server's experience with high-traffic sites?
- ▶ How big is the server?

The price of web fame starts as low as $14.95 per month. Some of the hosts will also allow you to register your domain at the same time.

save

Check out http:// sitebuilder.com, www. web.com, or www.weebly. com for inexpensive web design solutions. Cheap or even free, these companies offer templates for website design, free domain names, and a web host site. Weebly, for instance, offers a basic template for free; more complex, customized sites cost a fee. These sites are good for startup purposes until you have some income and business success to have a site designed to exactly meet your needs.

Chef, Sous-Chef, and Kitchen Help: Employees

No matter how small your specialty food business starts out, you may find a time when you need to hire help. Perhaps it is just temporary employees to help with specific projects—maybe a corporation has asked you to provide your product for a companywide event or you decide to have a booth at the large convention in the nearby city to sell whoopie pies to attendees—and you simply need some short-term, part-time help to get such a large order made and ready. If you plan to start bigger or have a retail storefront, you will likely want more permanent employees whether they are part time or full time.

Choosing employees—whether temporary or permanent—can be a deal maker, or breaker, for your growing company. You need a reliable team around you.

Who to Hire

Someone, whether yourself, a permanent staff member, or a temporary employee, will be needed to fill each of the following roles:

- ▶ *Office manager.* Oversees and coordinates employees and may also handle administrative, clerical, and office-supply duties.
- ▶ *Sales staff.* Sells from a retail site or on the phone and possibly networks to gain additional business.
- ▶ *Director of marketing.* Takes charge of advertising and promotion; often the person in charge of marketing also handles public relations and getting timely publicity to the media.
- ▶ *Bookkeeper.* Tracks all business expenses, and may also prepare tax returns; if you hire an accountant to do some of the higher-level tasks, you may be able to do the bookkeeping yourself.
- ▶ *Chef.* This is the chief foodie—probably you since food is probably what attracted you to the business to begin with.
- ▶ *Sous-chef.* This is the chef's assistant—the second-in-command that the chef entrusts with the implementation of the actual preparation. For example, perhaps the chef creates the recipe for the batter of the whoopie pie cakes and the filling; the sous-chef might be responsible for baking the cakes, making the filling, and putting the two together. Final taste and presentation are likely under chef's

tip

When hiring employees, consider the types of benefits you will be able to offer. These are an important incentive when choosing employees, as you will tend to field a better applicant pool if you offer benefits, whether that means paid vacation, sick days, personal days, flexible work schedules, trips to professional conferences, company-funded professional training, and health insurance, for instance. One way to do that is to join an association, like the local chamber of commerce, that might provide certain benefits for member employees at group rates.

▶ Be Upfront

When you decide it's time to hire employees, write a clear and detailed job description that outlines objectives. Use bulleted points to target the position's responsibilities, the working conditions, and the position's relationships to other jobs. Also clearly delineate the ideal candidate's skill set. This is critical because when you interview prospective candidates these will act as a type of checklist. It is tempting to hire employees who you immediately like, but do not necessarily have the strongest skills. Try not to let emotion take over when hiring employees. Of course, it is important that you and your employees' working styles mesh. Just remember to ensure they are also qualified candidates.

approval. Sous-chefs are most often employed by large restaurants and hotels, but if your business can afford it, you may find having a sous-chef-type position very helpful, especially if you, the business owner, are the chef.

▶ *Kitchen help.* This depends greatly on the size of your operation. If you have a large specialty food business that operates out of its own commercial kitchen and needs to fill significant orders on a daily basis, kitchen help from dishwasher to restocking person may be necessary to keep up with production. You do not want to pay the salary of a sous-chef or chef to have that person wash the dishes.

tip

Write your own job description. This will help you write the job descriptions for those you need to hire to do the things that aren't in your own job description.

Note that the above list is about roles, not titles. There is considerable variety in titles given to employees, but whether you use informal titles or more formal ones, the tasks are the same. Also don't feel like you absolutely need to hire a separate employee for each of these duties. It is more likely that you end up fulfilling all or most of these duties yourself.

Reaching Out to Candidates

Once you have determined the type of positions you need to fill, you will need to advertise these open positions. Don't skimp on this step. Cast your net as widely as possible to garner the best employees.

Advertising

Consider placing an advertisement in your local and regional newspapers. If the job you are filling is a more senior-level position, then also consider advertisements in larger newspapers as well as trade journals. These national ads, though, will be much more expensive, so plan on placing national ads only when the position warrants. National searches will likely attract candidates who will need to relocate so their salary expectations may also be higher in order to warrant a move.

Employment ads are typically placed in the classified section. Call your local paper and ask for an advertising representative who can walk you through the options. You may choose a simple three-line ad, or select a splashier, larger ad with a border helping to draw readers' attention. Be specific about your needs: hours, responsibilities, pay range, benefits, and qualities the applicant must possess (e.g., previous food experience). Finally, make sure no words are misspelled in this ad. Sounds simple, but, too often, classified ads make their way into print filled with typos. This will make you look less than professional. Run a spell check and make sure everything is in tip-top spelling shape. Here are additional venues in which to advertise your job availability:

► *Online newspaper advertising.* Check with the advertising representative at your local paper to see if the newspaper offers an online option. Most newspapers offer packages, including print only, online only, or both types of advertising. If the newspaper offers an online option, plan on placing an online as well as a print version of your advertisement.

► *Online job sites.* Online employment advertising on sites such as www.Craigslist.org and www. Monster.com is booming with more and more food businesses turning to it to find employees. However, you really are pulling in a national audience whether you intend to or not—make it clear in your ad where the job is located to weed out far-flung candidates who will likely not be moving 1,500 miles to take the job you have to offer paying $14 per hour.

► *Colleges and universities.* Colleges and universities often have their own newspapers as well as websites on which you can post your job openings.

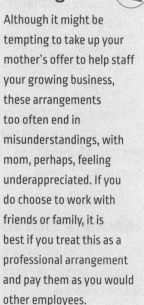

warning

Although it might be tempting to take up your mother's offer to help staff your growing business, these arrangements too often end in misunderstandings, with mom, perhaps, feeling underappreciated. If you do choose to work with friends or family, it is best if you treat this as a professional arrangement and pay them as you would other employees.

This is an excellent source for finding able candidates, especially for less senior positions.

▶ *Word-of-mouth.* Word-of-mouth is often invaluable in finding key employees. Let your vendors know that you are looking for employees. Call culinary schools in the nearest city and let upcoming graduates know that you have an opportunity for them to start getting the experience they need.

▶ Succession Planning

You have worked so hard to build your business. It's still small but it is successful and provides you with a good income. Or perhaps it isn't still small but has grown into a business that not only provides you with a good income but provides others with employment.

You won't stay in this business forever. Hopefully you will live a long life and perhaps it will be the thoughts of retirement that make you decide to call it quits—a large number of small businesses are started late in people's lives so this is a very realistic scenario. Or you decide to move on to something else. And of course, there is the possibility—however small—that you may have a fatal accident that removes you suddenly from your business.

In the latter case you may think, What do I care what happens with my business if I am simply no longer around? But we suspect you do care. That's why succession planning is important no matter what the ultimate reason you are no longer holding the reins.

William Vanderbloemen, in an article for business.com titled "From One Leader to Another: Succession Planning Tips That Build Better Business Leaders," offers the following couple of things to think about:

1. Admit that every leader is an interim leader. Some day your business will be gone altogether or you will be gone from it.

2. Write down a plan that states what things you do in your business right now that only you can do—name people who can take on these things and then talk with them about it.

Vanderbloemen claims that each year he reviews himself by asking one overriding question: Was I able to make myself less essential to the operation and growth of our company this year? However you decide to go about addressing your not being at the helm of your company forever, at least make some plans.

Interviewing

As you begin hearing from prospective applicants, you will want to read through their resumes and create a point system, perhaps from 1 to 10, giving 1s to unqualified candidates and 10s to top candidates. If you wrote an accurate job description, you shouldn't have many 1s. Nor should you have many 10s—dream candidates are rare. As you survey the resumes, use your rating system to decide which applicants to interview.

Interviewing Strategies

Plan on interviewing five to ten applicants for more senior positions, fewer for less senior openings. When an applicant arrives for an interview, have her complete an application form. These are available at local business supply stores such as Staples. You'll want to ask all candidates the same series of questions, ensuring a fair process. For help in formulating these questions, check www.job-interview.net. This site offers tips and advice about job interviewing and appropriate questions.

Take notes during interviews so you can review your notes later and winnow these candidates to two finalists. Ask these two for a second interview. Again, ensure fairness by asking both candidates the same series of questions. Take notes so you can access responses of both candidates after the interviews and make a final selection.

After the second interview, you will need to write an offer letter to the winning candidate, laying out your proposal, complete with pay structure and benefits. Once you and the applicant have signed the letter, you should let the other finalist know that the position is filled. Wait until the winning applicant has formally accepted before letting the losing candidate know the bad news. Too many times, the winning candidate has to decline the offer. Perhaps she received another offer and decides to take that. You will want to be able to turn to your second candidate.

Be as respectful of your candidates as you would expect them to be of the process. Always keep all candidates apprised of your time frame for hiring and let them know when to expect news. Always follow through, including making the tough calls, letting candidates know when they aren't selected. It's just part of doing business.

Pay

There are many variables to consider when paying your staff. For instance, in more urban areas of the country, pay tends to be higher. Compensation is also based on the employee's experience level and amount of responsibility. Median wage for a chef or head cook, according to the U.S. Bureau of Labor Statistics as of May 2014, is $45,390. An inexperienced worker with only moderate responsibility makes anywhere from $22,460 to $27,720. If you hire temporary help, hourly wages run around $10 per hour.

tip

If a local college offers culinary courses, part-time employees and interns should be easy to find. Contact the head of the department and ask about their internship program or whether you can help to create one.

Training

Be a good boss and take the time to adequately train your new hires and give them the benefit of the doubt for getting quickly up to speed. When they arrive for their first day of work, find a way to let employees know that you have been thinking about them and how to make this a good experience for both the new employee and the business. Show them how you like things done, where the things are that they need to perform the job they were hired to do, and the basics of your operation. You'd be amazed at how many employers show the employee to their station (desk, dishwasher, counter, whatever the case may be) and leave them to find the bathrooms or the break room on their own. There is simply nothing more frustrating for a new employee than being left to flounder. Plan on providing each employee with a detailed job description, delineating his or her responsibilities. Clarity and open lines of communication are key factors when dealing with employees.

Letting Employees Go

Unfortunately, if your business is open for any length of time you will likely find that at some point you will have to let an employee go for some reason.

Seasonal Workers

This is perhaps the simplest of all employee dismissal. You hired them with a specific timeframe and you let them go when that time frame ends. If your business, for example, is particularly busy for the Christmas season you may advertise to hire seasonal employees who start in early November to get up to speed on your products and your business by the famous "Black Friday" shopping day. When you hire these part-time, seasonal employees you make it clear that after the holiday—or the first of the year if a lot of gift certificates may get cashed in—their employment ends. Cut and dry, you both know that this is a short-term gig.

Layoffs

If your business is facing financial difficulties, letting go of employees is an important step. While you don't want to harm your business by not being able to make or sell your product because there is no one to do it, you also don't want to harm your business by retaining one of the largest business expenses there is—employees.

Layoffs are difficult but there are a few things to keep in mind:

▶ Employees are typically quite aware there are financial issues with the business.

▶ Layoffs typically allow for an employee to collect unemployment.

▶ Layoffs mean that you can provide a good reference for an employee, that you are not letting them go for lack of performance.

▶ Layoffs can be temporary—but don't mislead employees into thinking they will definitely get their jobs back. And vice versa, don't expect employees to be waiting in the wings for you to rehire them; they have their own needs and will find another job if possible. Sometimes a layoff can end if a big contract comes through, but contracts fall through all the time, so don't make any promises even if a contract is being negotiated.

Termination for Reason

Terminating an employee for poor performance, for not doing what he or she was hired for, for something egregious such as suspected (or proven) embezzlement, stealing property, etc., is where your retention of a lawyer comes in handy. Do not do these kinds of terminations without first consulting with a lawyer about how to handle the situation.

Then prepare yourself to do one of the unpleasant tasks of being a business owner. Nolo.com recommends the following:

▶ Hold the termination meeting somewhere private where the employee is comfortable unless you fear the employee may become violent.

▶ Prepare for the meeting by having a final paycheck, severance pay if applicable, and termination letter. Include date of termination and a list of things you have done to help the employee meet performance expectations.

▶ Start the meeting by informing the employee you are terminating employment. Don't add insult to injury by beating around the bush, exchanging pleasantries, etc.

▶ Explain your decision briefly. Don't go into extensive detail, which risks sounding apologetic or like you might be convinced to change your decision.

▶ Anticipate questions ahead of time and have answers—what should I do about my appointments later this week? Do I leave immediately? All these things should have answers.

▶ Unless the termination is for potentially criminal activity such as suspected embezzlement, end the meeting as positively as possible given the situation. Be sure the employee knows who to contact if he or she has further questions.

Talk with your lawyer in advance about the key things that you should avoid saying or talking about to help avoid a potential lawsuit. You never know how an employee is going to react, but you don't want to say something that may come back to you in court.

Unless you stay small and a one-person shop forever, unfortunately, terminating employees is a cost of doing business, so you can't hide your head in the sand about this topic. Be prepared to be professional at all times, even in this type of situation.

Vendors

Besides employees, at the heart of a successful business is a team of reliable vendors. It can't be overstated: Your business can be badly marred by even one bad vendor, if you can't fill an order because your supplier doesn't come through for you. You must do your due diligence when it comes to finding top-rate vendors.

Most of your vendors will be food-related. This means picking suppliers who have reliable products, especially when it comes to perishables.

Don't just let your fingers do the walking (or sliding, in the case of searching on your tablet instead of in the Yellow Pages . . .) when it comes to finding the best vendors. Research the vendors on your A-list, recording the following information:

▶ Vendor name, address, contact information
▶ Area of service
▶ Prices
▶ Lead times required
▶ Payment policy
▶ Refund policy

aha!

Whenever you introduce a new product or make a change to an existing product—making, for example, fall "pumpkin flavored" whoopie pies— let your staff be the first taste testers! When you have the recipe down, have a little celebration with the finished product. Let everyone join in being proud of the product.

▶ Discounts offered

▶ Specialty items/services

Most vendors will be willing to share client names with you so you can call and get testimonials that their product is top-notch and their delivery is reliable.

tip

If catering events is part of your specialty food business, consider joining the National Association for Catering and Events.

Professional Help

You will, at times, need to hire professionals, some just for consultations, others on a regular basis. Although these services sometimes arrive with a rather steep price tag, it is absolutely money well spent. These professionals will help to ensure the success of your specialty food business.

Professional consultants with whom any small business may work include:

▶ *Accountant.* A good accountant will be your single most important outside advisor and will have the greatest impact on the success or failure of your business. You will have to decide if your volume warrants a full-time bookkeeper, an outside accounting service, or merely a year-end accounting and tax-preparation service. Even the smallest unincorporated businesses employ outside public accountants to prepare their financial statements. Accountants typically charge $75 to $150 per hour. Be sure you keep your day-to-day books in good order, which will cut down on the amount of time you need to pay an accountant.

▶ *Attorney.* Finding the right lawyer early is critical. Although you hope never to need an attorney in an emergency or in negative circumstances, there are many other reasons to have a lawyer on your list of professionals before you have legal difficulties. Lining one up that you can trust and are comfortable with can be very helpful when things crop up. You may need your lawyer to help ensure that your business is in compliance with licensing and insurance regulations. A lawyer can also check documents before you sign them and help you draft documents like vendor and client agreements—you may have boilerplate agreements but hopefully you will get larger, complicated contracts that will go smoother with an attorney to browse them. And, of course, an attorney will

save

If you plan on doing most of your bookkeeping and are looking primarily for tax help, consider hiring an enrolled agent rather than an accountant. They can be found in the Yellow Pages or through the National Association of Enrolled Agents (www.naea.org).

▶ Choosing a Lawyer

Consider these factors when choosing an attorney:

▶ Will the attorney meet with you in person for an initial consultation—rather than a phone consultation?

▶ What is the attorney's background and experience? Specialty? Length of time in practice?

▶ Does the attorney have other retailers or food businesses as clients?

▶ Will the lawyer or paralegals perform the bulk of the work?

▶ Is there a charge for the initial consultation?

▶ What is the charge for routine legal work?

▶ Will the attorney work on a contingency basis?

▶ Is the attorney's website professional and appealing to you?

▶ Always check with your state bar association as well (www.abanet.org).

help resolve any legal problems that may arise. Attorney's fees range from $100 to $500 per hour.

▶ *Business consultant.* You may consider hiring a professional to analyze your business plan and check your ideas for feasibility. A good consultant can keep you from making costly mistakes. And it's always good to have a different but knowledgeable perspective.

▶ *Banker.* The right banker can be a tremendous asset to any small business startup. If you have a financial crunch—say a gap between having to pay for supplies to do a large contract and getting a deposit—a banker who has a good relationship with you may "float" you the required funds.

▶ *Insurance broker.* Another professional you will rely on is your insurance broker. Get one who will work with you. If you buy several types of insurance from the same company, you should receive a more attractive deal on the package.

Remember, investigate well and give careful thought to hiring those who will work with you. The time you invest in choosing your employees and other professionals will pay off in the end as you create a solid, smoothly running team for your business.

Don't Cook the Books: Accounting

E ven if you are famous for saying "I'm not good with finances," as a small-business owner, you need to at least know the basic dos and don'ts for managing your business's finances. In this chapter you will find suggestions for maintaining good cash flow, how to arrive at accurate pricing for your products and services, and how to figure the break-even point for your specialty foods business as well as a few simple tax tips.

Financial Statements

How you manage your financial assets may determine whether your business succeeds or fails. Your capital is not merely a collection of money and property, but a powerful business tool deserving your careful attention. Because going into business for yourself is such a risky proposition, it's helpful if your capital yields a higher rate of return than an ordinary investment would. Making capital work for you requires careful management of your business, especially of your current and future assets.

Financial management is an area many small-business owners neglect. They get so caught up in the day-to-day running of their businesses that they fail to take a good look at where their money goes.

It all starts with keeping good records in order to generate the financial statements that tell you exactly where you stand and what you need to do next. The key financial statements you need to understand and use regularly are:

- ▶ *Profit and loss statement* (also called the P&L or the income statement). This statement illustrates how much your company is making or losing over a designated period—monthly, quarterly, or annually—by subtracting expenses from your revenue to arrive at a net result, which is either a profit or a loss.
- ▶ *Balance sheet.* A balance sheet is a table showing your assets, liabilities, and capital at a specific point. A balance sheet is typically generated monthly, quarterly, or annually when the books are closed.

▶ Keep Abreast of Trends

All business owners need to keep on top of trends in their field, and specialty food is no different. From going green (organic food sources, packaging, etc.) to trends toward unusual and interesting ethnic foods, you can do some of your research standing in front of the local magazine rack.

Check out which magazine sections are largest and which magazines are thickest—the thicker the magazine, the more advertisers, which means the higher the circulation of the magazine, which means more readers, which means more people interested in that topic. Browse headlines for what those magazines are writing about.

▶ *Cash-flow statement.* This summarizes the operating, investing, and financing activities of your business as they relate to the inflow and outflow of cash. As with the profit and loss statement, a cash-flow statement is prepared to reflect a specific accounting period, such as monthly, quarterly, or annually.

You will need to review these reports regularly, at least monthly, so you always know where you stand financially and can quickly move to correct minor difficulties before they become major financial problems.

Paying Vendors

Although it might seem easy to organize cash flow as a startup since there might be very little initially, you may actually get so caught up in the other aspects of your daily routine that you forget to send an invoice or remind a customer that a payment is overdue. You might want to consider online invoicing tools like FreshBooks, or QuickBooks, which allow you to set up automatic reminders and acknowledgments. Even after your startup is built out and you are generating revenues, these tools will scale up with you and continue to keep your business organized. Many offer more features that you can add later on to handle larger volumes and projects so you never lose that efficiency that helped you from the start.

Keeping enough money flowing into a business is a universal concern, but the problem can be thornier in some types of specialty food businesses. For instance, if you are creating large orders for which you need to purchase supplies and pay employees well in advance of ever getting paid, you will want to make sure to require a deposit that allows you to purchase what you need and to set up accounts with vendors with terms that allow you to pay after you have received payment from your customer. A couple of other tips to alleviate cash-flow concerns include:

1. *Start with plenty of cash reserves.* Make sure that the amount you estimated in for your startup time period is realistic.

tip

Check out local community colleges, recreation departments, and other sources of noncredit classes where you can often find a financial class specifically aimed at those thinking about starting a small business. This is a great way to learn about financial reports and have an instructor to whom you can direct specific questions. And you get to meet other people in your same shoes who may become part of your trusted circle of small-business friends.

2. *Charge enough for your products and services.* Make a careful assessment of what you need to charge to turn a healthy profit. Otherwise, you will end up financially frustrated. In retail, you can always lower your prices if you find a particular product isn't selling. Remember that controlling costs is easier than trying to predict what your revenue will be. Once you look for additional ways to save money, you'll find them. That said, don't be "penny wise and pound foolish" and end up having your expense cutting cost you more indirectly.

tip

Whenever possible, save money by bartering services with other business owners. Perhaps you could provide food items for a meeting in exchange for brochure printing services or the creation of signage.

Pricing Your Products

The goal in pricing a product is to sufficiently cover overhead expenses (lights, heat, etc.) and cost of production (employee costs as well as materials) and generate an acceptable profit. The Vermont Specialty Foods Manual (published on www.vtspecialtyfoodbusiness.com) says you need to take all of the following into account when pricing your specialty food products:

▶ *Direct costs.* These are the cost of things tied directly to the production of your product such as ingredients, packaging, and wages for production workers.

▶ *Guaranteed sales.* This actually refers to product that you wholesale that does not sell but is returned by the retailer (i.e., the retailer's sales are guaranteed or they return unsold product).

▶ *Overhead costs.* Anything you need to spend to be in business that isn't directly tied to the cost of producing your product.

▶ *Profit needs.* What kind of profit (you can work with percentages but the dollar amount of your profit tells you how much actual money you will have to pay for these other things) does it take to keep you in business?

▶ *Distribution.* Even if you distribute yourself, it takes time, gas, wear and tear on a vehicle, and perhaps lease or purchase of a vehicle. If you use a distributor, you need to price their margin into your product markup.

▶ *Population served.* The income level of the population in the area in which you set up business (for local retail) will in great part determine how much you can charge for your products. If you want to charge more than the local economy will bear, you need to either set up shop somewhere else or focus on mail order where you can reach the demographic to whom you wish to sell no matter where you are physically.

You could still have a retail shop connected to your mail order business; you could charge lower prices in your shop to meet the market and call it your "factory outlet store."

▶ *Experience and reputation.* You do need to gain some reputation in order to charge top prices or you need testimonials from trusted, well-known people in order to come out of the box charging the highest tier of prices.

▶ *Price of similar specialty food products currently on store shelves.* You can under or overprice your product compared to other similar products but you had better back up your reasoning. If you price higher, your product better be that much better! If you price lower, your product likely will still need to be considered comparable to the higher-priced product. Find cheaper ways to package, print labels, distribute—cut corners in anything but the food itself!

> **warning**
>
> Even the smallest expenses add up. Supplying doughnuts and coffee at morning meetings with your staff is great for morale and helps to keep your team happy, but be sure to include a "doughnut allowance" when you calculate expenses!

Gift Certificates

One way to help with cash flow is to sell gift certificates. People love to buy gift certificates for gifts if you sell several different products—gift certificates allow the gift recipient to purchase what they like from your offerings. Or if you sell perishable foods, the gift recipient can purchase when they want the items and not have to eat them when given.

You can also offer gift certificates at discounted prices ($100 gift certificate for $75, e.g.,) or with a bonus (buy a $100 gift certificate and get a free $25 certificate) especially during the off season.

Gift certificates are a bit like money in the bank because often people wait months before cashing them in.

Markup

Industry markups vary widely, ranging from 100 percent and up. Markup rates depend mostly on overhead costs, but the health of the economy also affects them. In troubled economic times, markups (and therefore profit margins) will be lower. According to Jose Maria Pertusa (www.quora.com/What-are-common-gross-margins-or-just-retail-markup-for-a-high-end-food-store), "Brick-and-mortar gourmet food retailers operate at a 30 to 70 percent gross margin." Higher-value items, he says, have lower margins while lower-value items tend toward the higher margins.

Maintaining Cash Flow

Along with opening your business with adequate cash reserves, requiring deposits, and charging appropriately for your services, there are several other ways of ensuring good cash flow for your business:

- ► *Pay your company's bills on time, but do not pay early.* Keep your money in the bank as long as possible. The single exception to this rule applies if you have negotiated vendor discounts for early payment. Organize files by bills due in 10 days, 20 days, 30 days, etc. Choose a day, say Monday, and pay the bills due in 10 days. Then move the bills due in 20 days to the bills due in 10 days folder, the bills due in 30 days to the due in 20 days folder, etc. If you pay online, you could even change "10 days" to "due in two days" but don't cut it too close just in case you get distracted and don't get to your bills that day. Don't pay early but also avoid any late fees.
- ► *Make sure your invoices are clear, accurate, and timely.* When you do contract work, send invoices promptly. The difficulty of collecting an account increases in direct proportion to its age. Better yet, have the remainder of the bill (minus deposit) due when you deliver the goods. You hand a invoice, you get a check and mark the invoice paid. Always itemize invoices so clients know exactly what they are paying for.
- ► *Keep inventory and supplies to a minimum.* Carrying excess inventory can seriously impact cash flow. There are few things in this day and age that can't be had on almost a just-in-time basis.

Break-Even Point

We have cautioned you to make sure you have a substantial amount of operating capital, enough to last until you reach the break-even point. First you need to figure out your monthly costs that you will incur no matter what happens with the rest of the business.

▶ Loss Leader

Almost every business has one or two items that are huge sellers but whose profit margin is very low or even nonexistent. You don't want any of your products to lose money. But if you make giant whoopie pies with high-quality ingredients that are time consuming to carefully produce, you may find that this is what brings customers to your door but what you really make money on is that 90 percent of your customers can't resist buying six other higher-profit items when they come in for that whoopie pie fix. So your loss leader may be a great revenue generator even though it doesn't make much of a profit itself, but its biggest contribution is luring in customers who buy other things while they are in the store.

That is, you need to heat your retail shop and pay the person who runs your cash register no matter whether you produce a single piece of fudge or sell a single jar of salsa. So first, you need to:

- ▶ *Determine your monthly fixed costs.* Fixed costs are those that do not change, no matter how much product you produce (e.g., rent, utilities).
- ▶ *Determine your variable costs.* Variable costs are the costs of producing your various products, with varying quantities.
- ▶ *Estimate sales.* Estimating sales is difficult before you have ever even opened your doors but it can be done. You will want to determine how many people might come through your doors in a given time period and the average amount each of those customers might spend.

Determining the right margin to make an appropriate profit on all sales will be the key to how much you need to bring in in order to break even.

tip

Although you should strive for an accurate estimate, you may find that your final total differs from the initial estimate. For this reason, you should make it clear to your clients that your estimate is just that—an estimate. Make sure that this fact is stated clearly in your contract. Ensuring that you do not exceed your estimate by an unreasonable amount is an important part of your responsibility to your client.

Taxes

Managing your finances includes keeping a careful eye on your tax liabilities. These include:

► *Sales taxes.* Sales taxes are levied by many cities and states at varying rates. Most provide specific exemptions for certain classes of merchandise or particular groups of customers. Service businesses are often exempt altogether. Contact your state and/or local revenue offices for information on the law in your area so you can adapt your bookkeeping to the appropriate requirements.

► *Personal income taxes.* If you are a sole proprietor or partner, you will not receive a salary like an employee. Therefore, no income tax will be withheld from the money you take out of your business for personal use. Instead, you must estimate your personal tax liability and pay it in quarterly installments.

► *Corporate income taxes.* If your business is organized as a corporation, you must pay taxes on all profits.

warning

You must keep records to determine your tax liabilities. Regardless of the type of bookkeeping system you use, your records must be permanent, accurate, and complete, and they must clearly establish income, deductions, credits, employee information, and anything else specified by federal, state, and local regulations. You must keep complete and separate records for each business.

In addition to paying your own taxes, as a business owner and employer you will be responsible for collecting employee state and federal taxes and remitting them to the proper agencies. If you are a sole proprietor and plan to hire an employee, call the IRS at (800) TAX-FORM or access the information at www.irs.gov. Ask for a copy of Form SS–4. Also call your state tax agency.

Do not mess around with taxes. If you don't want to get familiar with the laws (and maybe even if you do), hire an accountant who will take care of your tax issues and let you know what you need to do when.

You may hire some individuals as independent contractors if, for instance, you cater the occasional event. According to the IRS definition, independent contractors are individuals who perform services for more than one firm, determine how the work is to be done, use their own tools, hire and pay their own employees, and work for a fee rather than a salary. If you hire independent contractors, you have to file an annual information return (Form 1099–Miscellaneous) to report payments totaling $600 or more made to any individual in the course of trade or business during the calendar year. If you do not file this form, you will be subject to penalties. Be sure your records list the name, address, and Social Security number of every independent contractor you hired, along with pertinent dates and the amounts paid to each person. Every payment should be supported by an invoice from the

► Tax Planning

Good tax planning not only minimizes your taxes, it also provides more money for your business. As an entrepreneur, you should view tax savings as a potential source of working capital. There are a few important rules to follow in your tax planning:

► Don't incur an additional expense solely for the sake of getting an extra deduction. This strategy is not cost effective.

► Immediately deferring taxes allows you to use your money interest-free before paying it to the government. Interest rates may justify deferring taxes, though doing so may cost you more taxes in a later year.

► If possible, claim income in the most advantageous year. If, as you begin your business, you are employed by someone else and expect to receive a year-end bonus or other additional compensation, you may want to defer receipt until the forthcoming year, especially if you will be in a lower tax bracket at that time (e.g., perhaps quitting your job to devote full time to your business).

contractor. Be warned also that if the IRS feels a worker whom you treated as a contractor should have been treated as an employee, you will be liable for payroll taxes that should have been withheld and paid, plus penalties and interest.

Deducting Expenses

Most small-business owners have some standard deductions they can claim to help offset taxes:

► *Home office.* You can deduct for all normal office expenses plus interest, taxes, insurance, and depreciation on the portion of your home that you use exclusively for business. To deduct, however, you must satisfy the following four usage criteria: exclusive use (the space is not used for anything else), regular use (occasional use doesn't qualify), business use (you must conduct business in that space), and administrative use (you must handle administrative

tip

All withheld income tax is treated as if spread equally over the calendar year, even when a disproportionately large amount is withheld in December. If you are required to make estimated tax payments, you should pay special attention to other techniques that may be beneficial, especially if your income is irregular or seasonal. Check with your accountant.

tasks at that location). Be aware that the IRS has traditionally audited a high percentage of taxpayers with home offices.

▶ *Computers.* A home computer used exclusively for business may qualify for appropriate business deductions or credits.

▶ *Automobiles.* Depending on which method you use, you may deduct for mileage or for mileage plus depreciation, garage rent, insurance, and repairs, among other expenses.

▶ *Travel.* You must stay overnight on business to claim deductions on air, bus, or auto fares, hotel bills, and incidentals like dry cleaning and gratuities.

▶ *Entertainment.* You can deduct 50 percent of your expenses, but you must maintain records of the following: amount of expenditure; date of expenditure; name, address and type of entertainment; occupation of the person entertained; reason for entertainment; and the nature of the business discussion that took place (general goodwill is not accepted by the IRS). Rules for deductions change frequently. You can also look online at www.irs.gov for tax updates.

▶ *Conferences and seminars.* The cost of the actual seminar is deductible, but deductions are no longer permitted for many of the expenses (e.g., food, lodging) incurred in connection with a conference, convention, or seminar.

▶ *Dues and subscriptions.* You may deduct these as long as they pertain to your field of business.

With proper management of your company's financial resources, you can greatly increase the probability that your business will succeed. Hiring the services of a competent bookkeeper to keep the day-to-day expenses well-recorded and an accountant to deal with the annual tax submissions is a great way to keep on the good side of the IRS and avoid nasty surprises.

When "To Market" Means Something Else

F ood business owners know a lot about the market—going to market, farmers' markets, that sort of thing. But if you want your business to succeed, you have to add a different kind of market to your vocabulary.

Why Marketing?

As you develop your business, it is important to market in order to grow your client base. Some successful business owners rely solely on word-of-mouth promotion—nothing can compare to a referral from a previous client. Others maintain informative websites or offer their client base a weekly email newsletter. As your company grows, you will determine which model works best. The pace at which you would like your company to grow will determine this, in part.

In this chapter we'll provide suggestions to guide you through the process of developing your strategy and help you evaluate the advertising media commonly used in the specialty foods industry. We'll also look at several other ways you can promote yourself and your new business, including the all-important social media, which we explore in detail in Chapter 12.

▶ A SWOT Analysis

Before you begin advertising and marketing in earnest, develop a road map of your marketing plans. This plan should include a SWOT analysis. SWOT stands for:

▶ *Strengths*. It is always useful to focus on this question: What are the unique and particular strengths of your business? How do these strengths set you apart from the competition?

▶ *Weaknesses*. Be honest—even if it hurts! What areas of your business are weak? Sometimes to even see weaknesses in your business you need to study similar businesses and compare. Develop strategies to combat these weaknesses.

▶ *Opportunities*. As the name implies, these are things that might benefit your company, now or in the future. For instance, perhaps a new retail center is opening in your area that is going to focus on locally owned small businesses. This is an opportunity for you to grow your business.

▶ *Threats*. List anything that might harm your business. Perhaps a big chain retailer is going to start making the same product you make (not nearly as well, of course, but still) or a new specialty food business is opening across town and also going to start offering cooking classes.

By focusing on these four areas and writing about them, you will help to focus your marketing efforts.

Networking to Business Success

Networking will be at the top of your list in terms of developing a strong client base—at chamber of commerce events, Rotary Club, honorary dinners. While you can't spend all of your time trotting around to every function within a 50-mile radius of your business, networking is essential if you want to develop new business.

Networking can help your business in many ways, but basically, if people have met you and know what services you offer, they may refer business to you or use your service themselves.

The Ins and Outs of Advertising

Print advertising covers a broad range, from an inexpensive advertisement in your local weekly newspaper to an ad in a glossy national publication costing tens of thousands of dollars. Lincoln Olive Oil Shop owner Rob Baker talked about the unique "Deal of the week" the Lincoln, Nebraska, daily paper does that he participates in. They sell $50 gift cards to his shop for $25, the paper gets the money, and the shop gets dollar-for-dollar advertising credit plus new customers and customers cashing in gift cards and spending more than the card is worth. Rob finds it a real win-win.

Even today in the online era, most businesses agree that an ad in the Yellow Pages makes good business sense. A line advertisement, simply listing your business name, is often provided free of charge when you connect your phone (if you have a land line). You can also opt for a display advertisement. These are the bigger, bordered ads in the Yellow Pages. There is a charge for these. If you do choose a larger ad space, be sure to include your logo.

warning

"Don't start cutting corners just to try to get your product into grocery stores," advises Winnipesaukee Chocolates owners Jonathan and Sally Walpole.

Regional magazines can be useful if you do corporate gifts or service for weddings. These magazines can be geared to topics related to your service (e.g., gourmet food, floral design) or aimed at readers in a certain region. An ad in a regional magazine might be a good tool for reaching upscale consumers. A regional business magazine ad would reach prospective corporate clients.

Advertising in national publications can be cost-prohibitive but it also can have big rewards if you can get the attention of customers who might order in large quantities. But be sure your business is prepared for the kind of business that might be generated from an advertising vehicle with national reach.

The Small but Mighty Business Card

Don't underestimate the power of this small but mighty marketing tool. Even in the computer age, a succinct, professional, printed business card is still critical. Consider it a diminutive brochure, especially if you opt for a trifold business card. Many businesses opt for this type of format because more information can be included than on a traditional business card, while the card remains small enough to be tucked inside a wallet or purse.

Include the name of your business, contact information (email, phone, fax, and website address, for instance), your name, specialization, your logo, and some testimonials from past clients. Always check with clients before using their testimonials and ask for permission to use both their first and last names.

Testimonials signed by John D. or Jane S. just don't have the same impact as those signed with a full name.

Always carry business cards. You might stand behind someone in the grocery store, strike up a conversation, and discover that she is starting to plan an event that your personalized whoopie pies might be the perfect dessert for. This is a key opportunity to pass along your business card.

You can buy blank business cards and print your own if you have a high-quality printer. But business supply stores print business cards relatively inexpensively. Choose the best stock (paper) you can afford. Likewise, if you are able to print in more than one color, then do so. For many clients, this will be their first impression of you and your business. Make sure it has a professional impact!

Information Brochures

The first question to ask is, do you need a brochure? They are not very costly, but you certainly don't want to spend money on something you do not have a use for. It is very discouraging to go through the time and money it takes to create and print a brochure, and then find yourself throwing a majority of the print run away a couple years down the road when you finally conclude that you didn't need a brochure after all.

The decision will be different for each type of business. Do you have a retail location in a tourist area that a visitor's center services with a rack of brochures to entice visitors to your place of business? That might be a great reason to have a brochure—to help drive customers to your business instead of hoping they just stumble on it.

Do you have the kind of specialty food business that the wedding industry might be interested in? Would it make sense to leave brochures with wedding planners or rental businesses or others in the wedding industry?

Like your business card, a well-designed, professional brochure can help cement your business's image. Prospective clients will make judgments about your company based on your brochure, so make sure that it is conceived and produced at the highest level possible.

To achieve this, plan on hiring a freelance graphic designer to help you develop this marketing tool. Tri-fold brochures are popular and allow you to include important information about your business. Photos of your products should be of the highest quality both in composition and sharpness. You may also want to include a photo of yourself. Because this marketing piece is making a critical first impression on prospective clients, consider hiring a professional photographer to help you obtain first-rate photos—he or she will know how to style things, what colors make things stand out. Even if you pay the photographer so that you own the photos, always be sure to credit anyone who does creative work on the piece itself.

Maximize your chances of success by making sure your company brochure matches the type of business you have. All materials should look professional, but if you are marketing to a budget-conscious group, a too-glamorous brochure can send the wrong message—and send potential budget-conscious clients running in the opposite direction.

aha!

Think a bit out of the box when it comes to marketing and advertising. Rob Baker of Lincoln Olive Oil Shop never imagined that he would abandon radio, minimize TV ads, and put all his marketing efforts into newspaper advertising given the general state of the newspaper industry.

warning

If you decide to try direct mail, don't try to use a rented mailing list more than once. These lists are "seeded" with control names so the list seller will know if you use the list more than once. Also, make sure you acquire your mailing list from a business in a related industry. This strategy will help target those potential clients most likely to use your services. Analyze the direct mailings you receive. What works, and what doesn't?

A word about online DIY design-and-print services like Vistaprint. While these services can be very helpful and are often inexpensive, talk to your local printer about giving you equally competitive pricing to get your business. Unless you have background in print design and want to spend your time on print design work instead of making and selling gourmet foods, let designers and printers do what they do best and you do what you went into business for to begin with.

tip

Provide the vendor with a brochure rack [available at Staples and other office supply stores] so your brochures don't end up in a messy stack on the floor somewhere—not professional!

Direct Mail

You may choose to distribute your brochure via direct mail. If you do so, make sure that your mailing list is well chosen. Consider renting mailing lists from associations to which you belong if that's applicable to your business. Mailing list rental can be expensive but if you choose the right lists, you will get a great return on your investment. And those new customers can become part of your mailing list.

Rental mailing lists are usually seeded with names of "spies" who will receive your mailing and 1) make sure it is what you said you were going to mail or within the parameters of what they allow to be mailed to their list and 2) that you are using the list that one time only. A person you mail to who comes into your store or orders from you online becomes your customer. But if one of the "spies" gets your next mailing even though they did not purchase from you and you did not rent their list again, you will likely be in breach of the mailing list rental contract.

Newsletters

Newsletters, if written in a lively and entertaining fashion, are useful marketing tools. Mail your newsletter to prospective, current, and previous clients, focusing on what is new in your business. Perhaps you have expanded your services or are offering a specially priced package. Keep the articles pithy and useful. Bulleted points are helpful to your client as are break-out boxes. Your clients' time is at a premium, so keep the articles brief.

You may likely choose to send your newsletter via email, an inexpensive and effective alternative to the slower "snail mail," although many organizations are still using the old-fashioned print newsletter so it must still be successful.

We'll discuss enewsletters later in this chapter.

Press Releases

Sending press releases is a fantastic and inexpensive method by which to boost your business. Send releases when you have business news to report—perhaps you have changed locations, released a new food product, or have some other event that is newsworthy. Newspaper and magazine editors need this so-called news "hook," so don't send press releases without news content. Editors won't run these.

A press release should include:

▶ *Release date.* Unless your release shouldn't be printed right away (in which case it should have an "embargoed" release date clearly stated), write "For Immediate Release" at the top.

▶ *Contact name.* Include your name, email, and phone number.

▶ *Headline.* Editors may change your headline, but give them an idea of the release content with a to-the-point, accurate, but somewhat tantalizing headline.

▶ *Dateline.* This is the city from which the release originates. So if your business is in Des Moines, then you should write "DES MOINES" in uppercase type. It should be placed as the first word of type before the press release text begins.

▶ *Text.* This is your news. Make it interesting to the editor so he will run it!

tip ⓘ

If you have a high-quality, stunning photo to accompany your press release, all the better. Although the newspaper may rewrite it, be sure to include a caption, name any people in the photo (with their permission), and give credit to the photographer or, if it's your own, mark it "courtesy of" and your business name.

Most magazines and newspapers prefer that press releases be submitted via email so staff does not have to spend time typing in releases sent via regular mail.

Although the editor may not choose to run all your releases, it is still worthwhile to email them off periodically. One reason for this is that the editor may turn to you when she needs a news source for a story on specialty food. Or, she may choose to use one of your releases as the framework for a feature story, which is a larger newspaper article.

The Power of Customer Service

Any business owner—or customer, for that matter—knows the one essential ingredient in running a successful business: customer service. You can be hard working and dedicated, construct a flawless business plan, and have a bottomless source of financing, but if you don't keep customers satisfied and coming back, your business will never succeed no matter what business you are in. Gourmet food is no different.

One of the best ways to keep customers coming back is to be constantly on the lookout for new ideas and for ways to improve the product and the service you provide. Toward that goal, consider the following:

tip

Don't immediately dismiss a customer's creative idea as wacky or not doable. Thoroughly investigate all ideas—not only will your customer be impressed that you took her seriously, but she will also be more understanding if you have to tell her it's not a feasible idea if you can back your decision up with some concrete evidence from your research.

- ▶ Invest in an hour (or more) with an industry consultant.
- ▶ Accumulate a group of testers that you can try new products on before deciding to bring them to market. Include the whole soup-to-nuts experience; that is, if your new whoopie pies will have unique packaging, present them to your focus group in that packaging.
- ▶ Constantly visit other gourmet food retailers or browse catalogs and websites to see what others are doing. Are they providing free shipping? Is the retailer in the next town using an iPad and the Square point-of-sale system? And how are those things impacting customer service?
- ▶ Attend as many arts-related functions as possible (e.g., arts exhibits, theatrical performances) to gather ideas.
- ▶ Join trade organizations (see list of organizations in appendix).
- ▶ Subscribe to at least one professional newsletter or journal.

Retaining Customers through Top-Notch Customer Service

You are sure to gain loyal customers if you are willing to do the following:

- ▶ *"Go to the wall" for clients.* You need to "make it right" at all costs. This could involve anything from handling last-minute emergencies to a willingness to "throw in" something extra for free, simply because the customer's experience with your product or service would be incomplete without it.
- ▶ *Offer customers something they can't get elsewhere.* Specialty food businesses have an innate "original" aspect of the work they do. More and more, customers want "different" and "unusual."

▶ *Make customers feel valued.* If you get a huge order from a customer or are regularly used by one customer for an ongoing service, consider doing something special for them—a discount coupon on other things they purchase from you, throwing in a box full of a new product you just brought to market. Or give them a gift certificate to some other aspect of your business such as cooking classes. Besides giving gifts, however, there are other ways to make sure customers know they are appreciated. A simple note with a personal message to convey thanks, congratulations, or birthday wishes can mean a lot, as can a phone call.

▶ *Think less in terms of services and more in terms of problem solving.* Work with customers on budget restrictions or special timing or how to get products to them in another city or whatever.

Giving Back to Your Community

Besides providing excellent customer service, earning (and keeping) the goodwill of clients and the community is important. Volunteering your company's help in planning charitable events or donating to your customers' favorite charities will win you many friends in the community.

▶ The Win-Win of Charity Work

The main impetus for your donations or volunteer work should be because you believe in the cause you are supporting and want to donate in some way. However, volunteering and donating for a charitable cause can have business payoffs in the long run. If you donate some of your specialty food items to a charitable event, make sure at the very least there is a sign beside your food station with your name on it. Better still is if you can leave business cards and/or brochures so that anyone attending the event who likes your food knows where they can find you.

While you may think when you first start up that you can't afford to give away to charitable causes, if you limit your donations and choose activities that give your business exposure to the maximum number of people who also support that cause, you will have spent a lot less on some good marketing than other avenues would provide for the same dollar amount.

Supporting charitable activities that give your business exposure is often referred to as "cause marketing"—having your business name associated with a charitable cause.

Building Your Image

Your image—the way your company and its services are viewed by the public—is very important. Some, therefore, will direct much of their advertising and promotion dollars toward building a good company image. You will have to decide how much you can afford to spend to establish, improve, and maintain your image. Increased revenues may be able to compensate for this expenditure.

Most important by far, however, is what your product says about your business. The quality of the specialty food items you produce is the most powerful shaper of your company's image and reputation.

Don't forget that small details also reflect on you and your company.

Traditional Media with a Digital Twist

Social media and electronic delivery of traditional media is taking on new dimensions all the time. From LinkedIn to Facebook, enewsletters to eblasts, tweets to blogs, Instagram to Snapchat and everything in between, no business can afford to ignore social media marketing and communications. However, before you dive in, it is also important to think through all the options, decide which work best for your business and your schedule, and tie them all together to back up each other's message wherever possible. In other words, you shouldn't just "do" social media because you are supposed to in today's world—you should pick the things that work for your business and post things that hold meaning.

Much of traditional media—newsletters, for example—are still used prominently in the business world. However, they are now typically generated digitally and transmitted electronically rather than in print on paper by post. Sometimes, depending on your typical customer base and their computer expertise, companies offer their materials both ways and let the customer decide whether to get their news, ads, brochures, or whatever—in print or electronically.

Enewsletters

An enewsletter is perhaps the most basic way to communicate with clients—it incorporates a standard format that most people are comfortable with (the newsletter) and integrates it with the digital format that is part of most people's everyday life (email). Newsletters that are sent via email are a great way for businesses to keep in touch with their customers. An email newsletter is like a little reminder to your customers that you are there and waiting

► Netiquette

Email, like any customer interaction, requires good etiquette. The last thing you want to do is offend a customer. Here are some guidelines:

► Never use all uppercase letters; it is considered the equivalent of shouting.

► Spell-check your emails. Just because email is quick, it doesn't have to be sloppy. Not as much of a problem when you are emailing with friends and family, but not professional when you are engaging potential clients. Also, check that the "autocorrect" function hasn't "corrected" your email to be inaccurate.

► Be enticing but also give an accurate sense of what your email is about in the subject line.

► Create a signature for your email so that every email you compose automatically includes your business name, address, phone number, and email address so the recipient can quickly see how to contact you.

► Keep your messages short and to the point. If you are including "articles" in your enewsletter, provide a capsule version of the article and a link to your website where a longer version of the article is available. For those interested, you also get a chance to get them to your website.

to fulfill their or their friends', families', and associates' needs. Do it on a regular basis, keep it short, and offer something like tips, coupons, recipes, or information on new products in each issue and your subscribers will look forward to your e-news popping up in their already overcrowded email box.

There are two key things to keep in mind about an enewsletter:

1. *Creating a newsletter is time consuming.* Just because enewsletters are cheaper to send (no printing, no mailing costs) doesn't mean you don't need to spend time pulling the newsletter content together. Think carefully about whether a newsletter at all is right for your business and whether the time it takes to pull it together will bring you a return of equal value.

2. *You need to solicit subscribers.* Sending enewsletters out unsolicited is considered "spam"; spamming is not only illegal but it creates ill will with your potential customers. But once you create a useful, readable, information-packed newsletter that might even contain a coupon or special or even a giveaway, people will readily sub-

scribe. Post it on your Facebook page and other places that might gain wider attention and more subscribers.

Press Releases vs. Event Listings

Press releases, also called "news releases," should be just that—news. If you have a piece of news to send to the media, by all means do it. A new hire, an expansion of your business into a new market segment, relocation, and accolades for you or your business are all news items about your business. News sources love to get press releases via email; attachments are usually fine but you should check with each publication you plan to send to and submit accordingly.

Event listings are not news and should be directed to the calendar or events section. Many online event calendars can be updated well in advance.

tip

Keep an archive of your news releases on your website—it's easy to do and is a great way for the casual browser to check you out.

Social Media

E newsletters are great communications vehicles, but the place where real creativity is taking place is in the world of what is actively known as "social media." Social media outlets present a fantastic opportunity for all small-business owners to meet and engage with targeted audiences full of thousands of potential customers. The cost of entry into this marketing channel is often only your time—however, don't underestimate the cost of your time! If used correctly, participating in social media will help your business grow through powerful word-of-mouth campaigns. But beware. It can suck a lot of time out of your day.

tip

"Twitter drives customer service in the digital age."
—*Harvard Business Review* online "Your Company Should Be Helping Customers on Social" by Maher Masri, et al., 7/15/15

To get started, there are a few things you should set up right away:

► *Facebook page.* Like anything that has been around for a few years, people's use of Facebook is changing and Facebook itself keeps making slight changes. Facebook keeps trying to engage more business uses, so pay attention to those and determine if they work for you. Some food businesses that make lunches, dinner-to-go, and bakery items post their changing menu every day on Facebook, allowing followers to plan to stop by on their way home to pick up a ready-made meal.

► *Twitter.* Twitter has a more instant, fun feel to it. While you don't have to be a stand-up comedian and post entertaining tweets, lighthearted and to the point (inherent in its 140-character limitation) is the name of the Twitter game.

► *Pinterest.* Definitely start a Pinterest account and post gorgeous pictures of your beautiful food items. Get friends to start to follow you, and some of their friends will start to follow you. Post enough interesting things and Pinterest users you don't know at all will start to follow you.

► *YouTube channel.* This is probably most useful to food businesses that offer cooking classes or if you want to show how you make your products so unique.

These social media accounts will become useful tools for you to interact with your audience.

Here are eight tips on using social media to your advantage:

1. *Before you start any social media outreach, define your target audiences.* How old are they? Do the people in your audience tend to be more female than male? What groups, organizations, or associations are they likely to join? Are they foodies? Or just people who like to eat healthy or unique foods? Think about the kind of people you market to and want to use your business—then hang out with them via social media outlets.

2. *Once your target audiences are defined, locate them online.* Search Facebook, YouTube, Twitter, and Pinterest for groups, organizations, channels, or discussions that would contain the people you are looking to meet.

3. *Use social media search and organizational tools to help you find your audiences.* Some sites like Facebook and YouTube have great, built-in search functions that will help you find your audience. To find your audience on Twitter, try using external sites like www.Twibes.com.

4. *Once you've found your audience on these sites, join their groups and lists so that you can follow the ongoing conversation.* Do not jump right in with a sales pitch! Listen instead. Learn the etiquette and major players. Spend some time just following along.

5. *After you're familiar with the etiquette and people involved, jump into the conversation when and where appropriate.* Do not hide who you are or the company you represent. Become a regular voice in the conversation and offer your friendly expertise to others. Invite people back to your website and social media accounts to see what it is you do and offer.

fun fact

"People under 35 spend almost four hours per day on social media . . . the volume of tweets targeted at brands . . . has grown 2.5 times in the past two years. The percentage of people who have used Twitter for customer service leapt nearly 70 percent between 2013 and 2014."
—*Harvard Business Review* online "Your Company Should Be Helping Customers on Social" by Maher Masri, et al., 7/15/15

6. *Once you're a regular voice in the conversation, don't be shy about doing a little promotion.* Contests, giveaways, and raffles can be great tools for audience interaction and promotion of your products. People will love the chance to play in your contest and will invite friends to join in the fun.

7. *As your audience grows, stay creative.* Invent new ways to engage your audience and encourage them to invite their friends. Continue to avoid hard sales pitches. People do not forward commercials to their friends. They forward value.

aha!

Management tools like SocialOomph can schedule updates and get engagement stats to help keep up with your social media and estimate its impact.

8. *Finally, do not try to do everything everywhere.* Sometimes it seems there will soon be as many social media platforms as there are websites. To try to maintain a presence on all of them is unsustainable. Focus on the top two or three that have proven to contain the largest number of people in your target audience.

Remember, social media provides you with the opportunity to meet your audience—not sell to your audience. People do not join these social media networks to find marketers. They join and participate for friendly interaction and the value that it adds to their day. Provide that friendly interaction, and watch your audience grow!

Blogs

Blogs, a shortened version of "web log," are typically personal and short, diary-like entries that touch on a specific topic. Perhaps you went to an event trade show and found out about a great new technique you are going to try in the next product you introduce. Or maybe you went to a seminar on whipping cream and want to share what you learned.

Like websites, there are templates, mostly free, available to make the blogging process simple—you sign up, create your blog, write your entries, and the template sets up an archive for you. Tumblr, WordPress, and Blogger are a few more popular blog platforms. Some website template services, like Weebly, offer blogging as an option with your website.

You don't have to be a bestselling writer to write your own blog. But if writing really isn't even a distant strong suit for you, consider hiring a writer to help you with it. Create a draft in Word, email it to your writing professional, and he or she can make it zing—and probably edit the grammar and proofread it, also. It's worth the small fee that an hour or two a week (or however often you do your blog) will cost. You pay an accountant to check your numbers, why not pay a writer to check that you sound just right to your target market?

Try to include both pictures and perhaps links to sites with further information in your blog. Again, use it to engage potential customers but don't use it as a strong selling tool. This is your chance to be personal with existing and potential clients. Give them some good information, and even if they don't become immediate customers, they may use you to cater their event or they may remember you kindly and tell their friends who are looking for a specialty food source to check out your blog.

► Enter the Blogosphere

Blogs are essentially online journals or brief newsletters, sometimes with more than one author. You may find blogs useful for networking, brainstorming, and simply commiserating with other food business professionals. Check out The Nibble online specialty food magazine's blog (http://blog.thenibble.com) for an example.

And like websites, no one will know you even have a blog unless you tell the world. Be sure to use phrases in your blog and mark keyword tags that help your blog appear when people search that word or phrase. For example, if you are writing about that whipped cream seminar, be sure to use the phrase "whipped cream" several times in the body of the blog or make sure to list the topics in the "tags" function.

You can link your blog to your Facebook and LinkedIn pages as well, so your friends and acquaintances on those sites will know when you've posted a new blog entry. It can appear with some initial teaser copy, enticing them to click on the link.

tip

Facebook itself has a "facebook for business" page at www.facebook.com/business that walks you through the steps for setting up a page for your business, including what is permissible and what is not.

Facebook

Facebook started as a way to communicate with your network of friends. However, not only have people always used it to promote their businesses but Facebook itself has been offering ways to make the social media platform business-friendly. And friends "like" websites that they want to support. So definitely create a Facebook page for your business but use it sparingly for directly promoting your product.

stat fact

"Some retailers have been able to increase sales conversions 10 to 15 percent by tailoring their social media content based on customers' previous purchases, according to McKinsey Research."

—*Harvard Business Review* online "Your Company Should Be Helping Customers on Social" by Maher Masri, et al., 7/15/15

A HubSpot blog (http://blog.hubspot.com) puts it best: "As a business on Facebook, you want to compel not repel customers." They show a great graphic that highlights things to do and not do. One key piece of advice is to follow the 80/20 rule—in this case, 80 percent of your posts should be social, and only 20 percent pertain to your business/products. Do respond to customer interactions within 24 hours. And, like with all social media, keep your posts short. Suggested frequency of posting is once to four times a week. This should go without saying, but do not write fake comments for your posts.

Postings to your Facebook wall might include some fun tidbits you learned about a new type of mustard or the region from which it comes, or some blooper packaging experiment you did.

Check out the pages of other food-related businesses and see how they are using Facebook to their advantage.

LinkedIn

LinkedIn is thought of as the Facebook of the business world. The general advice is to make your LinkedIn page more formal than a Facebook page might be. This is where people might go to see your resume, client list, a "serious" picture of you (i.e., a formal headshot, not the picture of your cat sleeping across your head).

LinkedIn is almost definitely going to be the more likely place your business is exposed to the corporate world if, for instance, your products include something that could be used for corporate gifts. However, no one can see more than the most basic information about you without your approval of a "connection" with them.

Twitter

A Twitter account for your business may be best used as an extension of a blog. You can send quick messages of up to 140 characters, a "tweet," to your subscribers. "Found the greatest fair trade coffee to use in next batch of macaroons—check the Macaroon Mania website for details!" or "Stop by the store Wednesday evening six to eight for tastings of our latest chocolate bars paired with red wines from WineBar. 123 Front Street" might be messages that promote your service while also offering benefit to the reader.

Photo-Sharing Platforms

Food is great for photo-focused media. The following are useful platforms for sharing images of your great products especially when they are being used in real-life ways and not just part of a photo shoot!

Pinterest

While there are loads of photo-sharing social media platforms from Flickr to Imgur to Tumblr and probably some being created as you read this, Pinterest seems to have landed as the most useful of them all, especially for things that are particularly visual and can be well captured in a close-up photo.

When you sign up with Pinterest, you can start a pin board themed by flavor (think "spicy" or "lemon"), food (yams, beef). Friends sign on to follow your pins. If you are looking for an idea (holiday whoopie pies, for example) you can search the topic on Pinterest and scroll through photos gathering ideas.

Instagram

Self-defined as "a fast, beautiful and fun way to share your life with your friends and family," Instagram is an image-driven version of Facebook (now owned by Facebook). Snap a picture and post it to your social network platforms. A key feature is that you can play with the appearance of the photo with filters. Instagram might be a good way to share images of your work or ideas that you find.

tip

Twitter—where "tweets" can only be 140 characters or fewer—is a more casual and personal media outlet like a blog and is referred to as a "microblog." You can post an image with your tweet.

Snapchat

Snapchat is another image-driven social media platform. The basic idea is that you snap a picture, add a caption, and send it to a friend—and it disappears in a few seconds after they open it.

More social media outlets are coming down the pike every week. The important thing to keep in mind is to use the ones that work best for your business. Don't let them work against you—like attaching a "hashtags" to an image but the hashtag is already taken so when someone searches it they come up with someone else's images. Definitely don't feel like you have to be involved in all of them. And especially don't overwhelm yourself so that you are spending more time keeping up with social media tweets and posts than you are in developing new business! You're in business to make and/or sell gourmet food, not to create social media posts.

Appendix
Specialty Food Resources

Just as you can never have too many cooking utensils from which to choose, you can also never have too many resources. Therefore, we present for your consideration the following resources for you to check into, check out, and harness those that seem useful to you as you prepare to make your mark in the specialty food industry. While these resources will get you started on your research, they are by no means the only sources out there. We have done our research, but events, websites, and businesses in the ever-changing specialty food market move, change, fold, and expand. As we have repeatedly stressed, you need to do your homework—but here's a jumpstart as you get out and start investigating.

Books

Creating a Thriving Business: How to Build an Immensely Profitable Business in 7 Easy Steps by George Horrigan (New York: Morgan James, 2013)

The Daily Entrepreneur: 33 Success Habits for Small Business Owners, Freelancers, and Aspiring 9-to-5 Escape Artists, S.J. Scott and Rebecca Livermore (Irvine, CA: Entrepreneur Press, 2014)

Directory of Convenience Stores, find it at www.retailbuyers.net

Easy Gluten-free Nutrition Advice and Recipes, Academy of Nutrition and Dietetics, Tricia Thompson, MS, RD, and Marlisa Brown, MS, RD, CDE, CDN (Chicago: Academy of Nutrition and Dietetics, 2011)

From Kitchen to Market, Stephen F. Hall (Chicago: Kaplan Business, 2000)

Marketing Guidebook: The guidebook of the supermarket industry lists over 1,300 retailer chains and wholesalers in the U.S. and Canada along with 1,500 specialty distributors and brokers. Information to help sell products to supermarkets. Find it at www.retailbuyers.net.

Start Your Own Business, Sixth Edition: The Only Startup Book You'll Ever Need, The Staff of Entrepreneur Media (Irvine, CA: Entrepreneur Press, 2015)

Start Your Own Food Truck Business, Second Edition, The Staff of Entrepreneur Media, Inc. and Rich Mintzer (Irvine, CA: Entrepreneur Press, 2015)

Start Your Own Microbrewery, Distillery, or Cidery, The Staff of Entrepreneur Media, Inc. and Corie Brown (Irvine, CA: Entrepreneur Press, 2015)

Conferences

Allergy and Free-From Show (www.allergyshow.co.uk). Specialty show in the U.K. specifically promoting dietary concerns for those who need to live "free from" ingredients like eggs, dairy, nuts, gluten, etc. Originating in London, the show is expanding to Liverpool, Germany, and Scotland.

Atlanta Foodservice Expo (www.atlantafoodserviceexpo.com). At the Georgia World Congress Center annually in the fall, bringing together all sectors of the restaurant, food service, and hospitality industries showcasing the latest products, technologies, and services.

Free From Food Expo (http://freefromfoodexpo.com). A European free-from trade event with distributors, manufacturers, importers and exporters, and information on packaging and process technology.

Food Ingredients (Fi) (India, Asia, South America…), *FiGlobal* (www.figlobal.com). A series of exhibitions in Asia, Europe, Latin America, and the Middle East for learning about food ingredients from all over the world.

Prepared Foods' New Products Conference (www.preparedfoods.com). The premier food and beverage event for gaining valuable insight into global new product introductions, culinary advances, and emerging consumer trends; the 2015 conference was in Palm Beach, Florida.

Retail Week Tech & Ecomm (https://techecomm.retail-week.com). In the U.K., an annual event created to bring together the best minds across disciplines in current retail changes and challenges.

United Fresh Produce Event (www.unitedfresh.org). In Chicago, annual conference of the fresh produce segment with exhibits and education sessions on business management, produce marketing, supply chain logistics; held in conjunction with the Food Marketing Institute and the International Floriculture Expo.

Consultants

Mintel (www.mintel.com). Offices in London, New York, Sao Paulo, Shanghai, Singapore, Belfast, Munich, Chicago, Sydney, Tokyo, Mumbai, Kuala Lumpur, and Toronto.

Magazines

Any of these magazines' websites can be searched online by the magazine name. Most sites have great information and many offer the ability to look through the current magazine in a digital edition from their site.

Baking Business—www.bakingbusiness.com

Cakes & Sugarcraft—www.cakesandsugarcraft.com

Cooking Light—www.cookinglight.com/magazine

Cooking Wild—www.cookingwildmagazine.com

Cook's Country—www.cookscountry.com

Cook's Illustrated—www.cooksillustrated.com

Diabetic Living—www.diabeticlivingonline.com

Farm and Table—http://farmandtablenm.com

Food and Wine—www.foodandwine.com

Food Business News—www.foodbusinessnews.net

Food Network Magazine—www.foodnetwork.com/magazine.html

The Gourmet Retailer—www.gourmetretailer.com

Saveur—www.saveur.com

Taste of Home—www.tasteofhome.com

Organizations

American Association of Candy Technologists, 711 W. Water Street, P.O. Box 266, Princeton, WI 54968, (920) 295-6969, www.aactcandy.org

American Bakers Association, 1300 I Street N.W., Suite 700 West, Washington, DC 20005, (202) 789-0300, www.americanbakers.org

American Cheese Society, 304 West Liberty Street, Suite 201, Louisville, KY 40202, (502) 583-3783, www.cheesesociety.org

American Culinary Federation, 180 Center Place Way, St. Augustine, FL 32095, (904) 824-4468, www.acfchefs.org

American Institute of Baking, P.O. Box 3999, Manhattan, KS 66505, (800) 633-5137, www.aibonline.org

American Pie Council, P.O. Box 368, Lake Forest, IL 60045, www.piecouncil.org

American Society of Brewing Chemists, 3340 Pilot Knob Road, St. Paul, MN 55121, (651) 454-7250, www.asbcnet.org

Association for Dressings and Sauces, 1100 Johnson Ferry Road, Suite 300, Atlanta, GA 30342, (404) 252-3663, www.dressings-sauces.org

Culinary Institute of America, 1946 Campus Drive, Hyde Park, NH 12538, (845) 452-9600, www.ciachef.edu

Food Processing Suppliers Association, 1451 Dolley Madison Boulevard, Suite 101, McLean, VA 22101, (703) 761-2600, www.fpsa.org

FDA Center for Food Safety and Applied Nutrition (CFSAN), 5100 Paint Branch Parkway, College Park, MD 20740, (888) 723-3366, www.fda.gov/aboutfda/centersoffices/officeoffoods/cfsan/

Grocery Manufacturers Association, 1350 I Street, Suite 300, Washington, DC 20005, (202) 639-5900, www.gmaonline.org

Institute of Food Science Technology, 5 Cambridge Court, 210 Shepherds Bush Road, London, W6 7NJ, UK, 44 (0)20 7603 6316, www.ifst.org

Institute of Food Technologists, 525 W. Van Buren, Ste. 1000, Chicago, IL 60607, (312) 782-8424, www.ift.org

National Honey Board, 11409 Business Park Circle, Suite 210, Firestone, CO 80504, (303) 776-2337, www.nhb.org

Organic Trade Association, 28 Vernon Street, Suite 413, Brattleboro, VT 05301, (802) 275-3800, www.ota.com

Snack Food Association, 1600 Wilson Blvd., Suite 650, Arlington, VA 22209, (703) 836-4500, www.sfa.org

*Specialty Food Association, (*646) 878-0301, www.specialtyfood.com

Specialty Foods Group, 6 Dublin Lane, Owensboro, KY 42301, (800) 627-1902, www.specialtyfoodsgroup.com

Packaging

Bags and Bows (www.bagsandbowsonline.com/retail-packaging/home)—Retail packaging

Crown Cork (www.crowncork.com)—Brand-building packaging

Encore International (http://encoreintl.com)—Creative custom packaging

First Impressions Packaging (http://firstimpressionspackaging.com)—Boxes, bags, gift boxes, tissue, and eco-friendly packaging

Jenn David (http://jenndavid.com)—Logos, packaging, print collateral, websites

Pacific Bag (http://pacificbag.com)—Coffee bags and stock and custom packaging for pet food, tea, and specialty food

ULINE (www.uline.com)—Shipping supplies and packaging

Glossary

A.Q.: "As quoted"—often used on menu items that are market priced

Back of the house: Restaurant phrase referring to the kitchen, dishwashing, and prep areas as well as the employees

Blog: An online journal or newsletter, usually with more than one author

Bond: An insurance contract used by service companies as a guarantee that they have the necessary ability and financial backing to meet their obligations

Boomers: People born between 1946 and 1964

Break-even point: The point at which your company neither makes nor loses money

Brix scale: A measurement for the density or gravity of sugary liquids

Candy thermometer: For measuring the temperature of boiling sugars or oils, goes up to 400 degrees F

Caterer: A company retained to provide food (and usually beverages, too) for an event

Chafing dish: A variety of portable cooking container used to either heat or cook food with a direct heat source; typically comprising a pan set on top of a pan of water so that the heat source is not directly on the pan containing the food

Chat room: On the internet, an electronic gathering place for people who share special interests, where they brainstorm and exchange ideas and information

Contingency plan: A written plan that is prepared in advance to address possible emergencies

Contractor: An individual or a company under contract to provide goods or services

Copyright: A form of protection used to safeguard original literary works, performing arts, sound recordings, and visual arts

Corporate planner: An individual who plans meetings for companies

Corporation: A separate legal entity distinct from its owners

Cuisine: A French term used to describe a specific style of cooking or a certain country's food in general, such as "Indian cuisine"

Culinary: Relating to the kitchen or cooking

Decant: To transfer liquid from one vessel to another, for instance to separate wine from any sediment

Demographics: The primary characteristics of your target audience, such as age, gender, ethnic background, income level, education level, and home ownership

Doing business as (DBA): A reference to your legal designation once you have selected a business name different from your own and registered it with the local or state government

Domain name: The address of an internet network

Dutch oven: A large, cast-iron kettle with a tight-fitting lid used for braising or stewing

Enophile: A connoisseur or lover of wines

Epicure: One who appreciates fine food and drink

Essence: Strong aromatic liquids created by distillation or infusion

Extrusion: In cooking, food extrusion is the process where mixed ingredients are pressed through an opening and cut into specific sizes.

Fancy food: Another name for "specialty food," which is defined as food and beverages that are made in small batches with high-quality ingredients

Finger bowl: Small bowl of warm water typically scented with lemon to wash fingers after eating shellfish or food eaten with hands

Flexitarian: "Semi-vegetarianism" where one follows a diet that is mainly plant-based with the occasional consumption of meat products

Fondue: Traditionally a dish of melted cheese served communally using long-stemmed forks to dip in breads, now also includes other types of melted dipping sauces such as chocolate

Free-from: The current terminology for the food segment that is "free from" certain ingredients or processes. Examples are milk produced from cows that have not been treated with growth hormones, meats that have not had dyes added to them, and gluten-free or dairy-free products. Some "free-from" consumers are following a diet because of medical conditions, others are just doing it because they feel it is healthier.

Functional foods: Foods that are considered to have a potentially positive health impact and go beyond fundamental nutrition

Garde manger: French term for the kitchen professional in charge of cold foods, salads, and hors d'oeuvres

Gluten: A protein found in wheat and other grains. Those with celiac disease are allergic to it. Others have been discovered to have a sensitivity to gluten which has given rise to the gluten-free trend.

GMO: Stands for "genetically modified organism," a controversial genetic engineering technique that, among other things, artificially selects for a desirable factor, like disease resistance or fast-growing or rot-resistant

Gourmet: Fine food and drink

High-touch: A term referring to events that require a high degree of care and handling

Homepage: The gateway to your internet website

Indemnification: A legal term meaning one party agrees to protect the other party from liability or damages related to an event

Infusion: The steeping of something in a liquid

Invoice: A document that indicates costs for goods or services owed by one individual or company to another

Irradiation: A method of sterilizing food using gamma rays

Liability: The legal responsibility for an act, especially as pertaining to insurance risks

Limited liability corporation (LLC): A business structure combining the tax structure of a partnership, yet protecting the owner from personal liability

Logo: A symbol used to identify or brand a business

Margin: Profit expressed as a percentage of the retail selling price (Margin = Profit/Retail Price). If a piece of candy sells for one dollar and it costs 50 cents to make it, meaning you make a 50-cent profit selling it for a dollar, the margin is 50 percent.

Markup: The amount added to the cost of goods or services to produce the desired profit

Matcha: Powdered green tea

Microblogging: A combination of blogging and instant messaging, where very short messages are sent to update subscribers about the microblog's topic. Twitter is the most well-known microblog vehicle, limiting the microblogger to 140-character messages.

Millennials: Those born from the early 1980s to the early 2000s

Nutraceuticals: A food having medicinal benefit

Newsletter: A marketing piece that offers short, newsy pieces about your business. Newsletters may be sent through regular mail or email.

Partnership: A business owned equally by two or more persons

Pâtissier: The kitchen staff member who prepares desserts, pastries, ice creams, etc.

Pescetarian: One who follows a predominately vegetarian diet but does eat fish

Proposal: A document outlining what a business will do for a client and the price at which it will be done

Relational database: A set of data structured so that information can be accessed across different databases

Rotisseur: The kitchen staff member who roasts, broils, or fries foods

Saucier: The kitchen staff member who prepares sauces, stocks, and perhaps does the poaching of meats, fish, or poultry

Site: The location for an event

Sole proprietor: Business structure description of a company owned by one person

Specialty food: According to the Specialty Food Association (www.specialtyfood.com), specialty food is defined as "foods or beverages of the highest grade, style, and/or quality in their respective categories. Their specialty nature derives from a combination of some or all of the following qualities: uniqueness, origin, processing method, design, limited supply, unusual application or use, extraordinary packaging, or channel of distribution/ sales."

Supplier: The individual or company that sells goods or services to another company; term often used synonymously with "vendor"

Target market: The section of the market, or group of people, to whom a company hopes to sell its product

Telemarketing: Using the phone to generate new sales or leads

Toque: The traditional chef's hat

Vendor: Most of the time in the specialty food business, "vendor" will refer to companies you work with that supply you with ingredients and supplies. If you cater events, "vendor" could refer to a company you hire to provide a certain aspect of the event catering—such as a florist for flowers for the buffet table or confectioner who makes the cake if baking is not your specialty.

Vendor agreement: A legal contract between food business professional and vendor

Venue: A site for an event

Website: A group of related documents posted on the internet, usually accessed through a homepage

Index